A Literary Traveler's Guide to the

GULF SOUTH

Bay St. Louis to Apalachicola

A Literary Traveler's Guide to the

GULF SOUTH

Bay St. Louis to Apalachicola

DIANE JONES SKELTON

A LITERARY TRAVELER'S GUIDE TO THE GULF SOUTH
BAY ST. LOUIS TO APALACHICOLA © 2022, 2024
SEAMARK STUDIO PRESS
Gulf Breeze, FL 32563

SEA MARK
STUDIO PRESS

Updates to the content of this book are available at
https://thegumbodiaries.wordpress.com/

Book Design: Diane Skelton

ISBN: 979-8-218-03890-8

For My Traveling Buddies,
Virtual, Real, and Armchair

TABLE OF CONTENTS

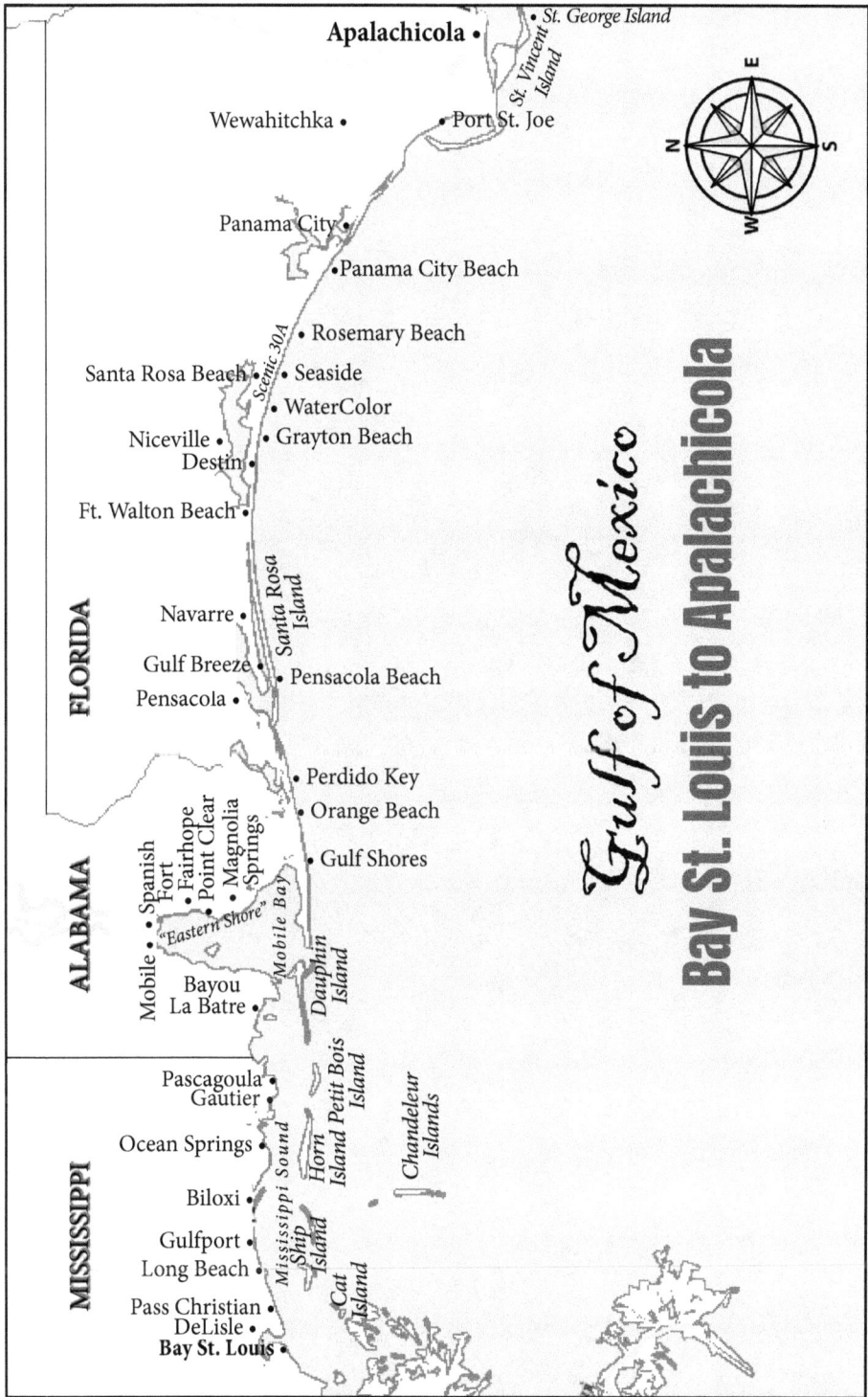

To the Literary Traveler

Before sophisticated satellites and hurricane tracking systems could pinpoint the precise path of a hurricane, I would listen to television weathermen reciting the names of exotic and enticing places. *"Hurricane warnings are out from Bay St. Louis to Apalachicola."* These melodious names sounded as strange to me as my hometown, Pascagoula, Mississippi, must sound to you.

The distance between Bay St. Louis and Apalachicola is 335 miles across three states — Mississippi, Alabama, and Florida. The area encompasses a vast and varied landscape and seascape. The marshes, swamps, bays, bayous, sounds, rivers, springs, waterways, moss-draped oaks, sandy beaches, clear emerald waters, and barrier islands along the Gulf of Mexico have inspired writers since the Spanish explorer Cabeza de Vaca visited the Apalachee tribe in 1526. No doubt the indigenous peoples who gave us tongue-twisting names like Wewahitchka, Apalachicola, and Pascagoula told their own stories even earlier. This book, however, is for literary travelers and tourists, and much less for historians, archaeologists, and scholars.

I invite you to join me and travel to hamlets, towns, and cities along the Gulf of Mexico. We'll visit where writers lived, worked, and placed their stories. From high-rise casinos to sleepy fishing villages, from sandy beaches to swamps and sprawling oaks, the writers and their works exemplify the importance of place in literature. The locations mapped in this book are located south of Interstate 10, beginning at Bay St. Louis, Mississippi. The route travels eastward, hugging the coastline along the Gulf of Mexico, ending at the Apalachicola River in Florida. The book's route is designed west to east, but traveling the exact route isn't necessary. For easy reference, places are listed in the index, along with titles, authors, and settings. Some towns are worth spending an entire weekend — others fill only an hour.

The writers included in this book have acquired literary achievement or recognition either with awards, reviews, or readership. Academic or journalistic works are included only when they are of great historic significance to the place. And, sometimes, one book or one author has put a town on *my* literary map.

As I wrote this book, two tropical storms entered the Gulf of Mexico simultaneously — an unprecedented event. Hurricanes and their aftermath appear in a surprising number of works described within these pages. Not one coastal town along this stretch has been spared. Novelists write of Camille, Frederick, Elena, Opal, Ivan, Dennis, Katrina, and most recently Michael — and that's only the major hurricanes in the past fifty years. But places, as much as natural disasters, have inspired volumes of interesting reading and provide fascinating landmarks to visit. Every location I visited offered more than my initial research had promised. For each new author I discovered, I read one of their books, short stories, essays, plays, or poems. And then, sometimes, the novels were so compelling, I couldn't stop with reading just one. I read the entire series.

Whether you're a writer, reader, teacher, traveler, or tourist, I hope this volume provides literary adventures offering you more than you ever expected along the Gulf of Mexico — from historic Bay St. Louis to mysterious Apalachicola.

Diane Jones Skelton
Gulf Breeze, Florida
August 2022, Updated November 2024, 2025

In a coastal region plagued by hurricanes from June to November, please call ahead or check sites on social media before visiting. Hours and days of operation may have changed. Pandemic restrictions may have been replaced or removed. For outdoor visits, bring sunscreen, insect repellent, and an umbrella because almost every day on the coast there's a chance of rain.

Mississippi Coast

Mississippi

The State of Mississippi reveres its writers and honors them with road signs, historic markers, and museums in homes as well as libraries. The state has officially developed a Mississippi Writers Trail and joins Alabama and Georgia in the three-state Southern Literary Trail.

Annually, Jackson, the capital city, welcomes tens of thousands of readers and authors to the Mississippi Book Festival, while the Oxford Conference For The Book attracts an academic crowd to the northern part of the state. Farther south, the University of Southern Mississippi houses the internationally renowned de Grummond Collection of Children's Literature.

The impressive and up-to-date Mississippi Writers and Musicians website, funded by a grant from the Corporation for Public Broadcasting and developed by a high school teacher and her students, exemplifies the value placed on literature by Mississippians of all ages.

The state earned its literary reputation from the works of William Faulkner, Tennessee Williams, Richard Wright, Margaret Walker, and Eudora Welty. These writers along with more contemporary ones have accumulated scores of awards that include William Faulkner's two Pulitzer Prizes and his Nobel Prize for Literature, Eudora Welty's Presidential Medal of Freedom for novels and essays, and Jesmyn Ward's National Book Award. Pulitzer Prizes for writers of fiction and nonfiction also include Welty, Tennessee Williams, Richard Ford, and editorial writers Hodding Carter III, Hazel Brannon Smith, and Ira B. Harkey. Natasha Trethewey earned the Pulitzer for poetry and served as the United States Poet Laureate. Trethewey also served as Mississippi's state poet laureate.

With so many literary superstars, it's no surprise Mississippi considers its writers as heroes. Until the last few decades, most of the accolades went to writers from the Delta and northern part of the state. More recently, the fresh, new voices of Natasha Trethewey and Jesmyn Ward expand the literary map southward. The Coast, as Mississippians call the area from Bay St. Louis to Pascagoula, has influenced its writers with rich settings, memorable characters, and a sense of place as soul-enriching as the fertile soils of the Mississippi Delta.

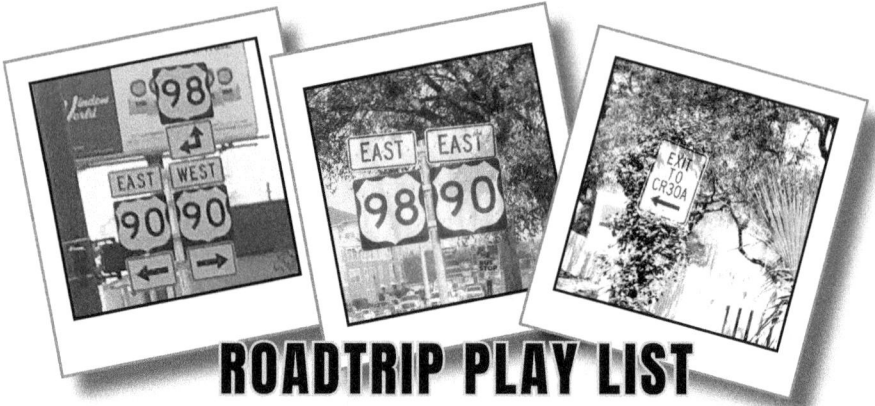

ROADTRIP PLAY LIST

"Pascagoula Run" (from Off to See the Lizard-1989) Jimmy Buffett

"Frank & Lola" (from Last Mango in Paris-1985) Jimmy Buffett

"Mississippi Squirrel Revival" (1984) Ray Stevens

"Apalachicola F-L-A" (1947) Bing Crosby & Bob Hope

"Southern Voice" (2009) Tim McGraw

"Gulf Breeze UFO" (2007) Ken Manning

"Forgotten Coast" (from Complicated Game-2015) James McMurtry

"Life is Just a Tire Swing" (from A1A-1974) Jimmy Buffett

"Running Bear Little White Dove" (1960) Johnny Preston

"Sweet Home Alabama" (from Second Helping-1974) Lynyrd Skynyrd

"Mississippi Girl" (from Fireflies-2005) Faith Hill

"Kryptonite" (YouTube Escatawpa Sessions-2021) 3 Doors Down

"Stars Fell on Alabama" (from Coconut Telegraph-1981) Jimmy Buffett

"Nothing but a Breeze" (Live at the Bijou Café-1977) Jesse Winchester

"Rhumba Man" (from Nothing but a Breeze-1977) Jesse Winchester

"Down the Road" (from Simple Life-1990) Mac McAnally

"Guitar Man" (from Clambake-1967) Elvis Presley

"Riders on the Storm" (from LA Woman-1971) The Doors

"Dauphin Island" (YouTube with So Brown-2010) Norah Jones

"Gulf Coast Girl" (2019) Caroline Jones & the Pelicanaires

"Island Rain" (Songs for the Saints-2018) Kenny Chesney

"Flora-Bama" (The Big Revival-2014) Kenny Chesney

"Mobile" Julius LaRosa (1954 hit re-released on Just Forever-2008)

"Let It Rock" (Rockin' at the Hops-1960) Chuck Berry

"Good Ole Boys" (Red River Blue-2011) Blake Shelton

"Gulf Coast Highway" (duet-1990) Emmylou Harris & Willie Nelson

"Gulf Coast Breeze" (single-2019) Allison Clarke

"Gulf Breeze" (Reflection-2010) Michael C. Lewis

South Beach Blvd. from downtown Bay St. Louis offers a view of the Bay of Saint Louis, the new bridge crossing the bay, and the $22 million municipal harbor. The city, nearly wiped off the map by Hurricane Katrina in 2005, has resurfaced as a lively beach town with cafés and shops.

BAY ST. LOUIS, MISSISSIPPI

Entering Mississippi from the west via Interstate 10, a highway sign welcomes travelers to drive along "The Stephen E. Ambrose Memorial Highway." That's official notice for every driver and passenger that writers are appreciated along this stretch of roadway and in the entire state. The designated highway ends at **Exit 13** with its intersection at **Mississippi Highway 43.** Take Mississippi **Highway 43-South** to see Bay St. Louis, the retirement home of America's favorite World War II historian, Stephen E. Ambrose, Ph.D. (1936-2002)

Ambrose, like so many other New Orleanians, chose this picturesque beach town as a second home. Ironically, Bay St. Louis, founded in 1699, is older than New Orleans. The population of around 13,000 enjoys a quaint downtown harbor with shops and lively restaurants. Much has been rebuilt since the destruction by Hurricane Katrina and before that, Hurricane Camille. Here, writers write about what they know, and they know about hurricanes, endurance, and survival, whether they were born here or moved here.

Though Ambrose grew up in Whitewater, Wisconsin, (where there's another memorial highway honoring him), he spent much of his life in New Orleans, where he taught at University of New Orleans. And for those who

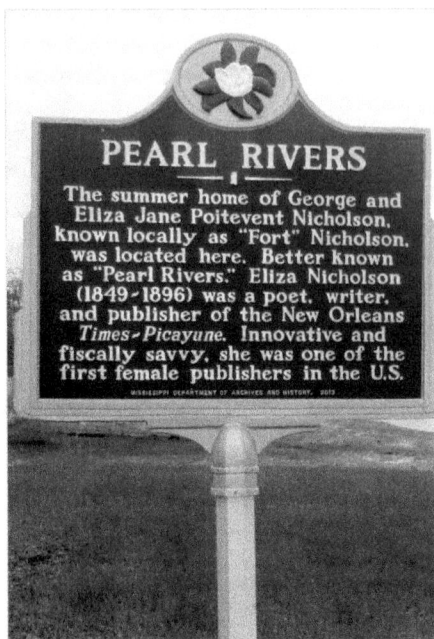

PEARL RIVERS

The summer home of George and Eliza Jane Poitevent Nicholson, known locally as "Fort" Nicholson, was located here. Better known as "Pearl Rivers," Eliza Nicholson (1849-1896) was a poet, writer, and publisher of the New Orleans *Times-Picayune*. Innovative and fiscally savvy, she was one of the first female publishers in the U.S.

MISSISSIPPI DEPARTMENT OF ARCHIVES AND HISTORY, 2013

A historical marker on North Beach Blvd. in Bay St. Louis stands at the site of the summer home of one of America's first female newspaper editors and the first president of the National Women's Press Association.

so often ask, "How did *New Orleans* get the World War II Museum?" the answer is simple – Stephen Ambrose. He spearheaded the campaign which began as a D-Day Museum and mushroomed into the National World War II Museum. Today, the massive campus located in the warehouse district of New Orleans takes a good two-day visit to appreciate every exhibit.

A bestselling author, Ambrose wrote more than thirty books, most of them on American history, exploration, and World War II. Most Americans, however, know him as author of the HBO television series "Band of Brothers," a Steven Spielberg-Tom Hanks production, and as the historical consultant for the film *Saving Private Ryan*.

After retiring as the Boyd Professor of History at University of New Orleans, he and wife Moira lived for twenty years along the beachfront in Bay St. Louis, sixty miles east of New Orleans. He called his two-story beach clapboard home "Merry Weather" after his award-winning biography *Undaunted Courage,* a story of Meriwether Lewis. Later on, the house doubled as the "headquarters" of the Ambrose-Tubbs family business of movies, films, books, and Stephen Ambrose Historical Tours. Though the Ambrose House no longer stands, a wooden stake marks the address at the vacant lot at **977 South Beach Blvd.** Ambrose seemed to like giving nicknames to his writing places. When he was writing the Eisenhower books, he worked from a one-room writing studio, complete with a sign outside the screen door which read "Eisenhowerplatz." (See page 12)

Bay St. Louis, Mississippi: 1699 Celebrating the first 300 Years, a catalog of historic homes published in 1998 by the Hancock County Historical Society, indicates Ambrose wrote from a writing studio on the second floor of Merry Weather. Though the couple owned a second retirement home in Helena, Montana, both are buried at **Gardens of Memory Cemetery, 630 Central**

Ave., Bay St Louis. Wife Moira, who died in 2009, was a former English teacher with a Ph.D. in English, and listened to her husband read aloud every word of the first drafts of his books.

Ambrose's personal library of books is on display at the **Hancock County-Bay St. Louis Library, 312 U.S. Highway 90.** The books were given to the library by his family following his death. The library is designated as a National Literary Landmark by United for Libraries, a division of the American Library Association. The library earned the distinction because Ambrose spent so much time there researching, in particular for his book *Nothing Like It in the World: The Men Who Built the Transcontinental Railroad, 1863-1869.* The library, which also has a nice READ poster featuring Ambrose's image, is one of nine such literary landmarks in Mississippi. The literary landmark status of another, just 25 miles away at **Beauvoir** at **2244 Beach Blvd.** in **Biloxi,** was rescinded in 2020.

A few blocks north from where the Ambrose house stood, a historical marker at **617 N. Beach Blvd.** indicates the summer home of famous female journalist Pearl Rivers (Eliza Jane Poitevent Holbrook Nicholson, 1849-1896). Eliza and husband George called their summer getaway in the Waveland-Bay St. Louis area "Fort Nicholson" because of a brick wall that surrounded it. The home, according to Hancock County historical records, featured broad wide galleries overlooking the bay. A Mississippi native, Nicholson edited what is now the *New Orleans Times-Picayune.*

She was the first female editor of a daily metropolitan newspaper and the first president of the National Women's Press Association. She added women's features to her newspaper and changed the way newspapers appeal to female readers. Eliza Nicholson's writing career began as a poet, choosing her nom de plume after the Pearl River, the major waterway near her birthplace of Gainesville, a ghost town about twenty-five miles west of Bay St. Louis. The town's site is now part of the Stennis Space Center. To the northwest about thirty miles, two towns honor her — Nicholson and Picayune. When railroads were bargaining their way through the Pearl River area, Nicholson, by then a famous newspaper publisher, was given the honor of naming a depot stop. She called it after her newspaper, and it remains the only Picayune in the U.S. (A picayune was a small Spanish coin, the cost of the newspaper in its early days).

The 1966 Paramount film, *This Property is Condemned,* based on the Tennessee Williams play, was filmed completely in Bay St. Louis. Reconstructed remains of the movie set are now home to the **Bay St. Louis Little Theatre, 398 Blaize Ave.** The movie's filming location only seems fitting because

On August 29, 2005, the homes of three well-known authors met their fate when Hurricane Katrina ravaged the Mississippi Gulf Coast.

1. Gone with the Wind . . . and RAIN

"Merry Weather," the Bay St. Louis home of Stephen Ambrose, America's favorite World War II historian, stood at 977 South Beach Blvd. Ambrose, the bestselling author of more than thirty books, might be best known for his work with Ken Burns and Steven Spielberg on *Band of Brothers* and *Saving Private Ryan*. Ambrose's true legacy, however, will be his guiding force in establishing the National World War II Museum in New Orleans. His home's name "Merry Weather" was a play on words from his popular book *Undaunted Courage* about Meriwether Lewis and the Lewis and Clark expedition. According to the Hancock County Historical Society, the Ambrose's Cape Cod-style house was built in 1985 on the site where St. Margaret's Daughters Home for the Elderly stood before being washed away by Hurricane Camille in 1969. The interior of the Ambrose home was open, featuring post and beam construction with white-washed walls. All three levels offered views of the beach. The exterior featured naturally weathered clapboard. When a visitor or newcomer asked for directions, it was often described as the "house with the windows." Between the house and the garage was a semi-tropical garden. Ambrose's writing studio and office were above the garage. After retiring as a professor at University of New Orleans, he and wife Moira lived at the location for twenty years. Ambrose died before Katrina, and Moira died in 2009, never rebuilding "Merry Weather."

PHOTO COURTESY HANCOCK COUNTY HISTORICAL SOCIETY

somewhere along this coastal stretch from New Orleans to Mobile, Tennessee Williams created a fictional Gulf Coast community of Sicilian immigrants for his 1950 play, *The Rose Tattoo*. Though the play's bayou village is never named, one character is a banana-hauler. The location most likely would be anywhere from Gulfport to Biloxi to Ocean Springs where Italian immigrants, many from Sicily, settled and bananas were traded. Williams, arguably America's greatest playwright, is a Mississippi native and lived in New Orleans, about sixty miles from Bay St. Louis. It's safe to assume Williams visited the Mississippi Coast, along with the scores of others hoping to exchange the heat of New Orleans for the breezes of the Coast. Williams was more specific when it came to the setting of his last performed play, *A House Not Meant to Stand*, which is set in a crumbling, haunted house in Pascagoula. The Southern Gothic two-act work is an expansion of an earlier one-act, *Some Problems for the Moose Lodge*. Tennessee Williams' marker on the Mississippi Writers Trail is in Clarksdale, his childhood home in the Mississippi Delta. (See Pascagoula, MS)

PASS CHRISTIAN, MISSISSIPPI

Discovered by French-Canadian explorers in 1699, Pass Christian is a harbor town with a population around 7000. The name is pronounced like the French — *Pass Christie Ann'*— with the emphasis on the "Ann." Locals just call it "The Pass."

Pass Christian was an antebellum resort community and boasted the South's first yacht club. By the Twentieth Century, mansions and vacation villas shaded by moss-draped oaks lined the beachfront. In 1912 and 1913, President Woodrow Wilson and his family wintered here in what became known as the "Dixie White House," a home destroyed by Hurricane Camille in 1969. In 2005 Hurricane Katrina wrecked almost all the other gorgeous, historic homes facing the six-mile-long beachfront. All but around 500 of the town's 8000 homes were demolished.

Host of television's "Good Morning, America," Robin Roberts (1960-) grew up in Pass Christian and returned to cover the hurricane's devastation for ABC News. Her high school was destroyed in Katrina. A Mississippi Historical Marker located at the school's former site on **West Second Street, about a block off Highway 90**, notes Roberts graduated from Old Pass Christian High in 1979.

A former college basketball player and ESPN sports broadcaster, Roberts is the recipient of a Walter Cronkite Excellence in Journalism Award and the Arthur Ashe Courage Award. She has written four nonfiction books, including her bestselling memoir, *Everybody's Got Something*, which tells the story of her battle with the rare blood disorder, myelodysplastic syndrome. Roberts' older sister, Sally-Ann Roberts, the bone marrow donor in Robin's battle with MDS, was the longtime news anchor for WWL-TV in New Orleans and is also an author. Robin Roberts won a Peabody Award, the radio-television-social media version of a Pulitzer Prize, for the coverage of her personal battle with MDS.

Margaret McMullan's *Aftermath Lounge* is a collection of ten short stories told from different perspectives describing Hurricane Katrina's onslaught of Pass Christian. McMullan (1960-) is the award-winning author of nine books including fiction, nonfiction, and an anthology. She writes full time from her home in Pass Christian. McMullan's historic family home on **Scenic Drive** where she was married was destroyed in Katrina. Her book, *Where the Angels Lived: One Family's Story of Exile, Loss and Return*, won the 2020 Nonfiction Award from the Mississippi Institute of Arts and Letters. The book is a personal account of her search for a relative and victim of the Holocaust in Hungary. She researched the book as a Fulbright Scholar living in Pecs, Hungary, and teaching at the University of Pecs. At times, the memoir draws personal parallels about Mississippi and Hungary and their burdens of history.

DELISLE, MISSISSIPPI

Four miles north of Pass Christian across the **Portage Bridge on Henderson Ave. at Whitman Rd.** is DeLisle, population between 1100 and 1200. Its most famous resident is Jesmyn Ward (1977-). Ward is the winner of the National Book Award for Fiction in 2011 for her novel, *Salvage the Bones*, and again in 2017 for *Sing, Unburied, Sing*. In her books, the fictional bayou community of Bois Sauvage is inspired by DeLisle. She calls nearby Pass Christian by the name St. Catherine. Though the names of the towns are fictionalized, Ward's descriptions of pines, oaks, Spanish Moss, marshes, bridges, blackberries, and pecans paint an accurate picture of this Mississippi coastal area. Growing up in DeLisle, Ward notes in *Salvage the Bones* that palm trees are alien, not native to the Mississippi Gulf Coast. In her writing she even captures the sweltering heat, laden with humidity. Some locations like Dedeaux Bridge sound authentic because of the use of popular surnames of the area. In fact, Ward's mother was a Dedeaux. Roads named after the early Dedeaux settlers of the area occur in three counties. **Rocky Hill Dedeaux**

Road, which has a bridge like the one in *Salvage the Bones*, is about **fifteen miles northwest of DeLisle**.

Driving along the shady two-lane roads winding through the countryside and marshland, travelers witness evidence of the poverty described in Ward's work. In her memoir, *Men We Reaped*, Ward weaves a perfect description of DeLisle, including its pesky gnats, into the narrative. Her younger brother, Joshua Dedeaux, was killed by a drunk driver and is one of the five deceased young men in the memoir. He is buried in **Saint Stephens Cemetery, 25220 St. Stephen Rd., Pass Christian**. Ward survived Hurricane Katrina in DeLisle, and in 2011 returned to DeLisle to live, write, and raise her family near relatives. While growing up, Ward attended nearby **Coast Episcopal School at 5065 Espy Ave. in Long Beach**; she now teaches at Tulane University in New Orleans. In 2018, the Mississippi Arts Council announced the establishment of a Mississippi Writers Trail which will include a marker for Jesmyn Ward.

LONG BEACH, MISSISSIPPi

Aptly named for its long beach vista, Long Beach is nestled between the older cities of Bay St. Louis and Gulfport. The first Europeans didn't settle here until the late 1700s. In the early 1900s the city gained fame as the "radish capital of America," but when long red radishes lost popularity and the Great Depression brought truck farming to a halt, the town transformed into a beach resort. The presence of Gulf Park College for Women, sometimes called Gulf Park By The Sea, enhanced its reputation as a cultured vacation spot.

While scores of hundred-year-old oaks in Long Beach were devastated by Hurricane Katrina, perhaps one of the most significant trees in literary heritage held strong. The 500-year-old **Friendship Oak, located across from the beach and Scenic Highway 90 on the University of Southern Mississippi campus** (formerly Gulf Park College for Women) took a beating but has recovered, much to the delight of poetry and nature lovers.

A famous poet taught poetry to college women under this tree in 1923 and 1924. Vachel Lindsay (1879-1931), who drew large crowds performing his rhythmic poetry across America, taught for seventeen months at Gulf Park, a newly opened two-year finishing school for girls. The college's first president recruited Lindsay, his old college friend, when Lindsay came to Gulfport to recuperate from surgery. As Gulf Park's poet-in-residence, Lindsay both wrote and taught poetry.

Young women learned poetry in a platform built around the Friendship Oak, in a cabin they called "the hut," and by moonlight and bonfires on the beach. At Gulf Park, the poet produced some of his best work after finding his muse, a student from Tennessee, who eventually spurned him. Lindsay preferred the celebrity lifestyle and declined a salary but asked for paid housing at Gulfport's luxurious Great Southern Hotel. He walked the three miles along the beach from the hotel to campus, wearing a dapper white linen suit, complete with white socks. During his brief stay at Gulf Park, scholars say he wrote some of his most creative poetry, experimenting with new styles. The Mississippi Gulf Coast is mentioned in his work written while at Gulf Park as well as the seven remaining years of his life. The "Pearl of Biloxi" reflects his love for his muse. "Billboards and Galleons" contrasts history and commercialism as the poet walks along the beach from the campus east to Biloxi imagining Spanish pirate ships on the right, advertising billboards on the left. To see the majestic oak that inspired poets and lovers, visit the 52-acre campus of what is now the **University of Southern Mississippi at Gulf Park. Enter from Highway 90 (730 Beach Blvd. E).** The tree is located near the front of the campus entrance between the Spanish Colonial buildings. A three-tier fountain from Lindsay's day still stands overlooking the beach. The Great Southern Hotel and the Anderson and The Strand, the movie theatres he frequented, are gone, but the Friendship Oak still stands, within steps of the Mississippi Sound where Vachel Lindsay loved to swim.

The bell and ornate archway overlooking the Mississippi Sound are remnants of the days when Vachel Lindsay taught poetry to young college women at Gulf Park College. The campus is now the University of Southern Mississippi at Gulf Park.

GULFPORT, MISSISSIPPI

A busy, international deepwater port city, Gulfport draws thousands of visitors for its beaches and casinos. Tourists barely notice the giant cargo ships in port hidden behind the impressive Mississippi State Aquarium and Jones Park with its Ship Island Lighthouse replica. Incorporated in 1898, Gulfport is Mississippi's second largest city, and a gateway to Gulf Islands National Seashore and historic Ship Island. And remember, it's pronounced GULF-port with the slow, Southern "uh" sound, not GOLFport like the game.

One of the most celebrated and admired poets of today wrote about Ship Island. Born in Gulfport in 1966, Natasha Trethewey, is a recipient of the 2007 Pulitzer Prize for Poetry, the 19th Poet Laureate of the United States (2012-2014), a Pushcart Prize winner for poetry, and Mississippi Poet Laureate (2012-2016). She lived her first six years in Gulfport and spent her childhood summers in North Gulfport (now incorporated into the city) with her maternal grandmother. Trethewey is one of three coastal writers to be included on the Mississippi Writers Trail and the only poet to ever serve as a poet laureate for both a state and nation at the same time.

Trethewey has earned professorships and fellowships at prestigious institutions including Yale, Harvard, Duke, Radcliffe, University of North Carolina at Chapel Hill, and Emory. The author of seven books, she currently teaches at Northwestern University and lives in Evanston, Illinois. But her work reflects her home state and the South. Trethewey's poetry, with its soft words and gentle but vivid descriptions, often deals with buried history and racial complexities. She won the Grolier Prize for Poetry for *Storyville Diary*, a collection of poems and photographs of prostitutes, many bi-racial, in New Orleans in the early 1900s. Her poetry collection *Domestic Work* won the Cave Canem prize for the best, first book by an African American poet in 1999. After Hurricane Katrina, Trethewey wrote a collection of essays, *Beyond Katrina: Meditations on the Mississippi Gulf Coast*. Her Pulitzer Prize-winning book for poetry, *Native Guard*, brings to light the Louisiana Native Guard, a group of African American soldiers stationed at the Union's Federal prison on Ship Island during the Civil War. While names inscribed in bronze on a plaque honor the Confederate prisoners, the black guards are forgotten, their bones washed into the Gulf. Trethewey filmed a reading of "Elegy for the Native Guards" from the book for Emory University's Poets in Place project at location on Ship Island, twelve miles off the coast of Gulfport.

ROCK-A-CHAWS TO SHUCKERS

Though there's a Viking, a greyhound, a timber wolf and a handful of lions and tigers on the road from Bay St. Louis to Apalachicola, most team mascots describe the area like an encyclopedia entry.

In Bay St. Louis, St. Stanislaus students cheer on the Rock-a-Chaws, a name derived from the Choctaw word for devil grass. That's those satellite shaped sand spurs that have brought down many a barefoot wanderer.

From the diamond to the court, the region boasts plenty of Dolphins, Sharks, Wahoos, Hurricanes, Gators, Rattlers, Admirals, Panthers, Pirates, and even a few Indians and Warriors.

Remembered more for their names than ticket box draw were semi-pro teams with colorful handles like Bay Bears, Surge, Sea Wolves, Bay Sharks, Mystics, Pelicans, and Beach Kings. Baseball fans are happy the Pensacola Blue Wahoos and Biloxi Shuckers are still hitting them out of the park. A Wahoo is a saltwater fish and "Shuckers" comes from the word "shuck." On the Coast, when folks open oysters with an oyster knife, they "shuck" 'em.

SHIP ISLAND, MISSISSIPPI

This barrier island's beauty offers a sharp contrast of its waters — the murky, gray Mississippi Sound on the north and the brilliant blue Gulf of Mexico on the south. Ship Island was split into two islands following Hurricane Camille in 1969 and is currently undergoing a restoration phase to rejoin the two. Historic Fort Massachusetts, built following the War of 1812 and used during the Civil War, is located on West Ship Island. The symbolism of the island's split is referenced in Natasha Trethewey's poem "Elegy for the Native Guards." The poem is included in *Native Guard*, which won the Pulitzer Prize for Poetry in 2007. (See Gulfport, MS)

A century before Poet Laureate Natasha Trethewey wrote of the Civil War and Ship Island, Major John William DeForest (1826-1906) offered a first-hand account of Ship Island in *Miss Ravenel's Conversion from Secession to Loyalty*, published in 1867 and notable because of his use of realism in fiction. The book is considered a major novel of its time. In the novel, Lillie, a young Southern woman with loyalties to the South, moves North with her father at the beginning of the Civil War. Her father is loyal to the North. Lillie chooses the wrong husband, and after a failed marriage and the war, becomes an abolitionist. An free electronic version of the book is available online.

As a volunteer Union officer, DeForest was stationed at Ship Island in 1861. He describes the island in *A Volunteer's Adventure*, his journal of the American Civil War, published posthumously. DeForest authored at least five other novels, two travel books, a history book, for a total of twenty books along with magazine articles, essays, short stories, and poetry. He is credited with coining the phrase "The Great American Novel." Never college educated, DeForest was a world traveler, living in Europe several years before the Civil War and returning to his home in Connecticut.

Louisiana writer Walker Percy (1916-1990) won the 1961 National Book Award for his novel *The Moviegoer*, which is on at least two of the Top 100 English-Language Novels lists. It ranks number sixteen on one. In the book, the main character Binx Bolling, a war veteran on a quest for greater self-awareness, travels the South in search of his new, postwar identity. On a daytrip with his girlfriend, Binx drives his red MG sports car from New Orleans along the Mississippi Gulf Coast to catch an excursion boat to Ship Island. Percy's novel, like Trethewey's poetry, conveys an importance of place, space, and history while describing Ship Island. Percy is recognized on the

Mississippi Writers Trail with a marker in Greenville, his boyhood home. Though he was a Louisiana native and spent his later years in Covington, Louisiana, he spent his childhood in Greenville with his cousin William Alexander Percy (1885-1942), a poet and lawyer who adopted Walker and his two brothers when they were orphaned. The Percy family has a long, literary history in Mississippi for at least four generations including novelist Sarah Anne Dorsey (1829-1879), and her two aunts, authors and publishers Catherine Anne Warfield (1816-1877) and Eleanor Percy Lee (1819-1849). (See Biloxi, MS)

"Ship Island," a short story by Elizabeth Spencer (1921-2019) is included in the Modern Library Classic's series *The Southern Woman: New and Collected Fiction*. The female protagonist in the story, subtitled "The Story of a Mermaid," is on a search for self-identity. Spencer's novel *The Salt Line* is set along the Mississippi Gulf Coast in the fictional town Notchaki during the rebuilding of the community after Hurricane Camille. Spencer, a native Mississippian, wrote nine novels, a memoir, a play, and seven short story collections. Her most famous work, *Light in the Piazza* written in 1960, sold two million copies and became a movie in 1962 and a Tony Award-winning Broadway musical in 2005. In the story, a mentally disabled woman traveling in Rome with her mother falls in love with a handsome young Italian man, who, in turn, wants to marry the daughter, despite her mother's efforts to explain her mental condition.

Though Elizabeth Spencer started out as a Southern writer, her world travels provided global settings in her later works. However, she was a charter member of the Academy of Southern Writers and considered herself a Southern writer. A Mississippi Writers Trail marker honoring Spencer stands in her hometown of Carrollton, in the Mississippi Delta.

Part of the Gulf Islands National Seashore, Ship Island sits eleven to twelve miles off the coast of Biloxi and Gulfport and is accessible by private boat or excursion ferry. Public ferries run from both Biloxi and Gulfport. The Gulfport ferry leaves from **Jones Park at 1022 23rd Ave.** (off Hwy. 90) certain months of the year. The Biloxi ferry, which runs fewer months, leaves from the pier behind **Margaritaville Hotel at 195 Beach Blvd.** (Hwy. 90).

LEAVE THE SAND

The stretch of beach along Mississippi's coast is the longest manmade beach in the world, measuring 26 miles.

ISLAND HOPPING

From the mainland, you can't see all the islands between Bay St. Louis and Apalachicola. Several are part of * **Gulf Islands National Seashore**, others are protected but uninhabited, and some are lively beach towns. Each island has its own unique history and characteristics. Working together, the islands form a barrier, protecting the coastline from hurricanes and natural erosion.

CHANDELEUR ISLANDS (MS)

Local fishermen spin tales of big catches at the Chandeleurs, located about 30 miles south of Biloxi. French explorer d'Iberville first anchored on the islands on the eve of the religious holiday, *La Fete de la Chandeleur* (Candlemas, the festival of candles or light). From 1848 to 2005, "light" shone in the form of a lighthouse on Chandeleur. All three were destroyed by hurricanes. The last one, listed on the National Register of Historic Places, disappeared in 2005 after Hurricane Katrina. According to LighthouseFriends.com, the "light" from Chandeleur saved at least two shipwrecked crews.

CAT ISLAND (MS)

During World War II, animal trainers and dogs inhabited the island in a top-secret training mission using family pets donated by patriotic Americans. The dogs were trained to track down the enemy by scent. The island's name is derived from the French *chat sauvage,* describing its raccoon population.

*SHIP ISLAND (MS)

Hurricane Camille split this island into two islands in 1969. Nature was trying to heal herself until 2005 when Hurricane Katrina widened the gap. Now, a $400 million project is rejoining the severed parts. You can take the excursion ferry or a boat and visit the Civil War prison site there, but no one spends the night.

* indicates part of Gulf Islands National Seashore

In the Roaring Twenties, a resort hotel and gambling casino stood on the Isle of Caprice, twelve miles off the Mississippi Coast. A storm blew in and cut the island in half. With more storms, the island began to erode and was submerged. Could it be thousands of visitors had picked the sea oats, leaving little vegetation to hold the land in place?

DEER ISLAND (MS)

This skinny island is so close to the Biloxi mainland you can see it from Highway 90. There's no public transportation to this 4.5-mile-long island (rent a kayak). If you can get to this island you can camp among endangered species (and alligators). It's a coastal preserve with nature trails managed by Mississippi Dept. of Marine Resources.

*HORN ISLAND (MS)

Now famous artist Walter Anderson rowed here from his home in Gautier to study, draw, and paint the wildlife. If you want to spend the night, you'll have to pitch a tent like Walter. Occasionally, a group of artists will boat out, sketch pads in hand, to study the same wildlife Anderson recorded in his logs.

ROUND ISLAND (MS)

From this island, the colors of the water seem to split – on the northside the Mississippi Sound water is gray; on the southside the Gulf of Mexico's open waters are sparkling blue. The remnants of the island's lighthouse which served mariners for 150 years was saved and portions relocated to Pascagoula. Visitors can tour the "top half" at a park on Highway 90.

*PETIT BOIS/WEST PETIT BOIS ISLANDS (MS)

It takes a boat to reach this part of the Gulf Islands National Seashore, but those who visit these pristine protected beaches rave about its beauty. French explorers named it Petit Bois (pronounced petty boy), meaning little woods. Hurricane Katrina inundated the island, killing most of the little forest.

DAUPHIN ISLAND (AL)

When French explorers landed, they found so many skeletons they called it Massacre Island. Chances are the bones were from an Indian mound destroyed by a hurricane. Eventually named for the Dauphin of France, this island is accessible by vehicle from Mobile on the Dauphin Island Expressway or the ferry. It has resorts, homes, two historic forts, public beaches, some pirate history, and surf good enough for a teenage Jimmy Buffett to learn to surf.

*SANTA ROSA ISLAND (FL)

This populated resort island is home to Pensacola Beach. The condos, houses, hotels, and restaurants are sandwiched between protected areas of the Gulf Islands National Seashore. Geronimo was imprisoned in Fort Pickens, on the western end. A toll bridge from Gulf Breeze gets you onto Santa Rosa Island. There's no toll on the eastern entry at Navarre but it costs to enter the National Seashore.

*OKALOOSA ISLAND (FL)

Technically this "island" is part of Santa Rosa Island, but locals call it Okaloosa Island. Follow the bridge (Highway 98) from Fort Walton Beach to see a bustling boardwalk, hotels, some secluded beaches and the Gulfarium Marine Adventure Park. If you're there at the right time, the island hosts a great Mardi Gras parade.

SHELL ISLAND (FL)

Across the "Pass" from Panama City Beach, parts of Shell Island belong to St. Andrews State Park. Visitors can reach the seven-mile stretch of island by private boat or the Shell Island Shuttle (boat). Shell Island is the most popular spot around for snorkeling. It's also a great place to see bottle-nose dolphins frolicking in the Gulf. But it's primitive — no restrooms, concessions stands, or camping.

ST. VINCENT ISLAND (FL)

This National Wildlife Refuge is accessible only by boat and home to several endangered species, including the red wolf. Florida Fish and Wildlife Conservation Commission regulates several official hunts here each year. In a "big game" hunt, 200 hunters chosen by lottery, use primitive weapons (muzzle-loading rifles or bow) to hunt for Sambar Deer. The deer arrived on the island from India in 1907, when the island's private owner was developing a "wildlife emporium."

ST. GEORGE AND LITTLE ST. GEORGE (FL)

Take the bridge from Eastpoint to this island with fewer than 1000 residents. No high-rises or chain restaurants here, just quaint shops, colorful beach houses and personal residences across from the dunes. The blend of marsh, clear Gulf waters, pristine white beaches, state park with nature trails, a lighthouse, and spectacular sunsets make it a photographer's paradise. During World War II, St. George Island was a practice range for B-24 bombers.

Navarre Beach on Santa Rosa Island boasts the longest fishing pier in the Gulf of Mexico, 1,545 feet long and 30 feet above the water.

BILOXI, MISSISSIPPI

From pulp fiction to poetry, romance to history, Broadway to the movies, literary travelers will find whatever their hearts desire in Biloxi. This history-rich city founded in 1699, is pronounced BUH-LUX-EE. That's *lux*, not lox. Say "LOX" and locals will immediately spot you as an out-of-towner. This vibrant bayside and beachfront town is home to a major Air Force base and snazzy casinos. The town was once known for its seafood industry, strip joints, the Dixie Mafia, and the Mad Potter of Biloxi, ceramist George Ohr. This colorful past, survival through major hurricanes, and today's lavish casino atmosphere make it perfect as a literary setting or an ideal getaway for a writer.

Avid popular fiction readers recognize Biloxi as the setting for several John Grisham (1955-) novels including *The Runaway Jury*, *The Confession*, and *The Partner*. *The Runaway Jury* and *The Confession* both mention **Mary Mahoney's Old French House Restaurant located at 110 Rue Magnolia**, a place frequented by lawyers, judges, and jurors. As one of Grisham's favorite places to eat, the restaurant owners annually send Grisham his favorite gumbo for Christmas. The restaurant posts Grisham's thank-you notes on Facebook. A native Mississippian, Grisham has homes in both Oxford, Mississippi, and Charlottesville, Virginia. After Hurricane Katrina hit, Grisham traveled to the Coast to check in on the owners of Mary Mahoney's. Grisham and his wife Renee established Rebuild the Coast Fund, a nonprofit that provided over $8.8 million for restoration after the hurricane.

Humorous mystery writer and *USA Today* bestselling author Gretchen Archer set *Double Whammy*, her first book in a multi-book series, at the fictional Bellissimo Resort and Casino in Biloxi. The location was inspired by the **Beau Rivage Casino and Resort at 875 Beach Blvd. (Hwy. 90)** according to a 2015 online author interview with Fresh Fiction. When Archer celebrated her 40th birthday with her family at the Beau Rivage, she went home a big dollar winner. After that, she began writing the casino series. Though the books are humorous, expert attention is paid to casino security procedures since the main character handles security in the fictional casino. The detailed research is especially evident in *Double Agent* (2019), book eight in the series. The plot deals with procedures for securing the casino and its millions of dollars as a massive hurricane approaches the beachfront casino. Biloxi is featured in several other books in the series as the home of the main character, Davis Way. The word "Double" is in every title. The cozy mystery series was first published by Henery Press. Her short stories "Double Jinx," "Double

Deck the Halls," and "Double Bluff" are also set at "The Beau," as the locals call Beau Rivage. Archer lives on Lookout Mountain, Tennessee.

In Greg Iles' (1960-) page-turning mystery *24 Hours*, the main character, a physician, checks into his room at the Beau Rivage for the Mississippi Medical Association's annual meeting. He's scheduled to be a lecturer at the event until the phone call comes that his young daughter has been kidnapped. Iles is the award-winning, bestselling author of the *Natchez Burning* trilogy. He grew up in Natchez, Mississippi, and still lives there.

Larry Brown (1951-2004), Mississippi novelist and short story writer sometimes compared to Faulkner, Hemingway, and Carver, wrote in a vivid, yet terse style. A Vietnam Marine veteran, he wrote while holding down a full-time job as a firefighter in Oxford. His collection of short stories *Big Bad Love* was made into a movie in 2001 and his novel *Joe* adapted for film in 2004. *Fay,* Brown's novel published in 2000, is set inside shady bars and massage parlors in Biloxi in the 1980s, a dark contrast to the glitz and glamor of today's bright-light casinos. Brown's awards include the Southern Writers Critics Circle Award and the Thomas Wolfe Prize. In 2018 the Mississippi Arts Council announced the establishment of a Mississippi Writers Trail which will include a marker for Brown.

Contemporary paranormal romance writer Katie Reus, a *New York Times* and *USA Today* bestselling author, set two books of her *Into the Darkness* series in Biloxi. Reus, also writing as Savannah Stuart, has written nine series and more than fifty books. A native Floridian, Reus lives near Biloxi. Women's detective fiction writer Karen White (1964-), a *New York Times* bestselling author of twenty-four books, set her novel *The Beach Trees* in Katrina-ravaged Biloxi. (See WaterColor and Apalachicola, FL)

USA Today bestselling author Carolyn Haines grew up in Lucedale, Mississippi, sixty miles northeast of Biloxi. Her mystery-thriller *Revenant* is set a few months before Katrina in Biloxi where a mass grave is discovered behind an old nightclub. The main character, a female reporter suffering the loss of her daughter, lives across Biloxi Bay in Ocean Springs. Haines is the author of more than seventy novels in various genre. (See Gautier, MS, and Mobile, AL)

In *The White Album,* a collection of essays by National Book Award winner Joan Didion (1934-2021), "On the Mall" describes Edgewater Plaza as a "good way to spend a day if you wake feeling low in Biloxi." Godchaux's, the exclusive department store she mentions is gone, but despite Hurricane Katrina's massive blow, the shopping center held on. Bruised but refurbished,

Edgewater Mall, as it's now called, boasts fewer live oaks yet retains its classic beachfront view at **2600 Beach Blvd. (Hwy. 90)**. With a hundred shops and stores and nearly a million square feet, the shopping mecca still offers a good way to spend the day if you're feeling low — or if it's raining.

When a young Neil Simon (1927-2018) joined the Army Air Force Reserve just before the end of World War II, his first assignment was Keesler Army Base, now known as **Keesler Air Force Base** (technically located at **4503 M St.** but locals will always tell you it's off **Porter Ave. at the end of Pass Road**). His experiences here were the basis for his Broadway play *Biloxi Blues*, made into a movie by the same name in 1988. The movie, however, was filmed in Arkansas. Simon wrote in his memoir, appropriately titled *Neil Simon's Memoirs*, that Biloxi is the hottest place in the world in August by twenty degrees.

Located at **2244 Beach Blvd. (Hwy. 90), Beauvoir** was home to Jefferson Davis (1808-1889), President of the Confederacy, following his imprisonment after the Civil War. It is the site of his Presidential Library. The National Historic Landmark covers fifty-two acres and includes the home, library, cemetery, and outbuildings. The cottage where Davis wrote *The Rise and Fall of the Confederate Government*, his fifteen-hundred page, two-volume apologia, no longer stands but has been replaced with a replica. The main house, Beauvoir, suffered extensive damage in two hurricane — Camille and Katrina — but has been restored. Brick fireplaces kept the footprint intact and historic photos in the National Archives provided reconstruction details. In 2021, eighty-five percent of the original house remains; the rest has been restored. The original owner, James Brown, designed the house as a summer home, and in doing so situated it to allow breezes from the Sound to Oyster Bayou to pass through. Informative tours are included with the admission price. Today's visitor needs imagination to recreate what it may have looked like with no traffic or Highway 90. What is viewed today as the front of the home was actually built as the back.

Beauvoir was designated a U.S. Literary Landmark by the American Library Association's United for Learning division. The status was rescinded in 2020. According to the tour guide, the literary distinction was originally bestowed for writer Sarah Dorsey (1829-1879), a novelist, and the second owner of Beauvoir. A Natchez socialite and wife of wealthy lumberman Samuel Dorsey, Sarah traveled in literary celebrity circles in the U.S. and Europe. Guides at Beauvoir say she was present at the first reading of Edgar Allan Poe's "The Raven" and also at one of Charles Dickens' salon readings.

Sarah Dorsey wrote six novels, four of which were published in book form,

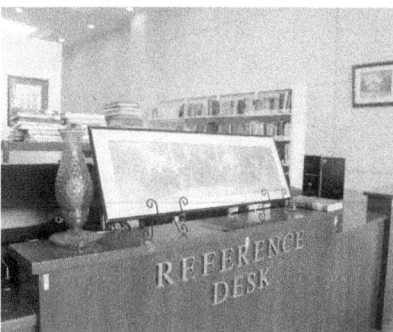

Beauvoir, the home in which Jefferson Davis lived following the Civil War, was owned by noted female author Sarah Dorsey. After his imprisonment, she invited Davis to live and write his memoirs at Beauvoir. Upon her death, he inherited Beauvoir. Now a National Historic Landmark, Beauvoir includes a presidential library, museum, rebuilt cottage-library where Davis wrote *The Rise and Fall of the Confederate Government,* and the home itself. Oscar Wilde once visited Beauvoir and would have been entertained in the parlor pictured above.

the other two serialized. She penned the biography of Louisiana Governor Henry Watkins Allen, a rare task for a woman at the time. Biographies were usually reserved for male writers. She came from the wealthy and literary Percy family — her two aunts were authors and publishers. Writers William Alexander Percy and Walker Percy are descendants.

Sarah Dorsey's husband died before the completion of Beauvoir. Fascinated with Jefferson Davis, she invited him and his entire family to live at Beauvoir following his release from prison. Dorsey and Davis' wife were both from Natchez and knew each other. Dorsey rented a library cottage to Davis and willed Beauvoir to him. Some scholars speculate that Dorsey was instrumental in Davis' completion of *The Rise and Fall of the Confederate Government*. One Beauvoir tour guide suggests she wrote much of it.

Often-quoted Irish poet and playwright Oscar Wilde (1854-1900) visited Jefferson Davis at Beauvoir in June 1882 while on a literary tour of America. Wilde described Davis' tome *The Rise and Fall of the Confederate Government* as a masterpiece and Davis as a "keen intellect" and the one American he wanted to meet, perhaps because of a family connection. Jefferson Davis knew Wilde's uncle (Wilde's mother's brother) who was a judge and lawyer in Louisiana. Wilde's first cousin, a captain in the Confederate Army, had died during the Civil War from dysentery. Wilde spent the night of June 27 with the Davis family at Beauvoir, entertaining the three Davis women — wife Varina, daughter Winnie, and cousin Mary — long after the elderly Jefferson Davis had retired for the evening. Guides at Beauvoir spin an interesting tale of Jefferson Davis' dislike for Wilde, and, as a result, how Davis' dog held Wilde at bay from strolling the gardens with the other guests.

One evening Oscar Wilde visited marked the eighteenth birthday of Winnie Davis (1864-1898), known as the Daughter of the Confederacy. Winnie lived with her parents at Beauvoir during the 1880s. Mother and daughter were both aspiring writers, perhaps inspired by meeting Wilde, and moved to New York. Both women wrote for *New York World* newspaper published by Joseph Pulitzer, a family friend who was married to a distant Davis cousin. Winnie wrote two novels, *The Veiled Doctor* and *A Romance of Summer Seas*, and a monograph, *An Irish Knight of the 19th Century: Sketch of the Life of Robert Emmet*.

Contemporary novelist Charles Frazier's historical novel *Varina* (2018) contains fictional accounts of Varina Davis' time at Beauvoir, narrated in conversations with James (Jim Limber), the "adopted" black son of Jefferson and Varina Davis. A statue of Davis with his young son Joe and Jim Limber is located on the grounds east of the library cottage.

On August 29, 2005, the homes of three well-known authors met their fate when Hurricane Katrina ravaged the Mississippi Gulf Coast.

2. Gone with the Wind . . . and RAIN

Built around 1840, the home at 1196 Beach Blvd., Biloxi, was one of the first vacation villas along the beach. It acquired its popular name, The Father Ryan House, when Father Abram J. Ryan, Poet-Priest of the Confederacy, lived and wrote there following the Civil War. Most locals and visitors recall the house as the one with the palm tree growing out of the front steps. When Father Ryan lived there, he'd walk along the beach to visit Jefferson Davis, who was living and writing at Beauvoir. Before Katrina, the house was listed on the National Register of Historic Places, noteworthy for its architecture. It had been renovated in 1885 by its owner T.W. Carter, a New Orleans architect. In its final years, just before Katrina, it was again a home for vacationers – this time for tourists, not as a second home. The Father Ryan Bed & Breakfast included rooms with symbolic names like those for Philip, a homeless orphan Father Ryan found living on the beach, and Jefferson, for Jefferson Davis. Hurricane Katrina destroyed the home, but the palm tree remained until 2014 when it was mistakenly cut down after a cold winter. Legend says the tree had been planted by Father Ryan for a grotto. What remains now is a vacant lot and a historic marker, its back depicting the palm tree growing out of the front steps. His most well-known poem is "The Conquered Banner."

Father Abram Joseph Ryan (1838-1886), the Catholic priest dubbed the "Poet-Priest of the Confederacy," completed his second book *A Crown for Our Queen* while in semi-retirement from 1881-1882 in Biloxi. The Greek Revival beach home where he lived and allegedly wrote "The Conquered Banner," his most famous poem, was destroyed by Hurricane Katrina in 2005. **A marker** where the former National Historic Landmark stood is located at the **intersection of Caldwell Ave. and Beach Blvd. (Hwy. 90)** between The White House Hotel and the Biloxi Lighthouse. Coastal residents remember the house as the one with a giant palm tree growing up through the front steps. **Father Ryan Avenue, one block north of Highway 90 runs east and west between Biloxi Upper Elementary School and the Biloxi Cemetery** (just south of Keesler). The priest, while living in Biloxi, would visit Jefferson Davis at nearby Beauvoir. (See Mobile, AL and page 29)

Prentiss Ingraham (1843-1904), a colonel in the Confederate Army, soldier of fortune, Buffalo Bill Wild West Show press agent, and fiction writer claimed to have written more than 600 novels. His pocket-sized "dime novels" included series on Buffalo Bill, Dick Doom, Merle Monty, and Buck Taylor. Sometimes called the King of Dime Novels, he also wrote under at least eight pen names and was a ghostwriter for Buffalo Bill Cody. The son of an Episcopal clergyman-author, Ingraham wrote "154 words every hour of every day for thirty-four years" according to an exhibit in the Dept. of Archives at the University of Mississippi. He died at the Beauvoir Confederate Soldiers Home in Biloxi and was buried at grave marker #62 at the cemetery, where 783 other Confederate veterans and their families are interred. Now known as the **Confederate Veterans Cemetery,** it is located on the grounds of Beauvoir, the last home and presidential library of Jefferson Davis at **2244 Beach Blvd. (Hwy. 90)**

WATER, WATER, EVERYWHERE

If it's got water, it's a wetland; how much and what kind makes the difference

Swamp – wetlands with trees, where high and dry land meets wet and underwater land

Bayou – a slow-moving swamp without trees, pronounced "bi-yoo"

Bog – spongy land where water hides below the surface, like pitcher plant bogs

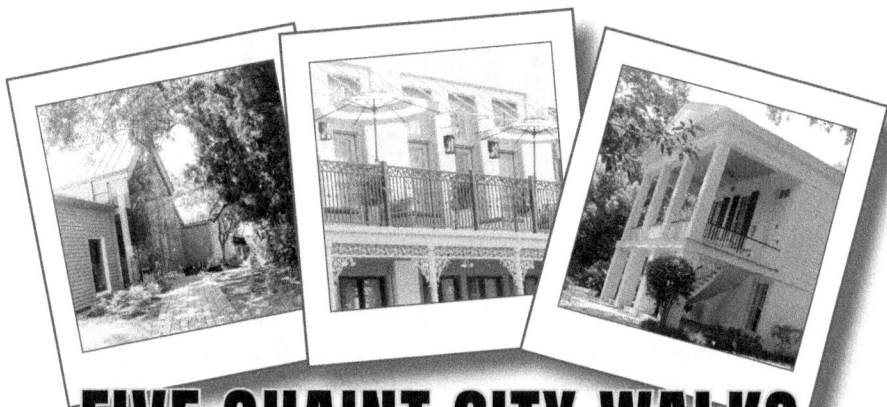

FIVE QUAINT CITY WALKS

DOWNTOWN OCEAN SPRINGS (MS)

Winner of the "Great American Main Street Award," the city offers a main street area with an art museum nestled among shady oaks, crooked sidewalks, bistros, bakeries, and eateries. Even the community center and the cultural center are artists' meccas. It's no surprise to see acclaimed national artists displayed in the galleries right beside accomplished local artists, a fitting tribute to this city that fosters art and artists.

OAKLEIGH GARDEN HISTORIC DISTRICT (MOBILE, AL)

Step back in time and stroll this historic residential neighborhood centered around Washington Square and dotted with shops, sidewalk cafés, and a popular Irish pub. The neighborhood developed around historic Oakleigh House, built in the 1830s, and includes hundreds of homes with architectural styles ranging from Creole cottages to Victorian to Greek Revival. It's also noteworthy for its lush landscaping, front porches, and sidewalks shaded by sprawling live oaks.

DOWNTOWN FAIRHOPE (AL)

No matter the season, colorful flowers bloom on every street corner in this artsy town. The city has its own horticulture and landscape department, which grows and plants the floral displays six times a year. Even the lampposts overflow with flower baskets and beckon pedestrians to walk around, shop a little, sneak into a gallery or antique shop, enjoy sidewalk dining, and visit the famous bookstore. Locals say more writers live here per capita than any other place in America.

QUAINT CITY WALKS

PENSACOLA'S PALAFOX STREET (FL)

The city's new downtown look merges the historic section, museums, and Palafox Street, a trendy main street beginning at the yacht harbor at Pensacola Bay and going north for blocks with fine restaurants, galleries, coffee shops, breweries, and unique shops. Pensacola takes the best from other successful downtowns – murals, bikes, scooters, artsy sculptures (pelicans and cubes) mingled with sidewalk dining to create a glitz and glamor destination street. Palafox was named one of the Ten Great Streets in America in 2019 by the American Planning Association.

APALACHICOLA HISTORIC DISTRICT (FL)

This casual coastal town is reminiscent of Florida before theme parks. It runs on Florida time, with one shop closing around three-ish, but there's no rush because all you need is daylight to enjoy the historic walking tour strolling by excellent examples of early Florida residential architecture. Outside the wonderful bookstore in downtown, dozens of monarch butterflies flutter by. Not far from downtown, the John Gorrie State Park Museum pays tribute to everyone's hero, the pioneer inventor of air conditioning. Stroll across from the museum and see a historic church, monument, and roundabout. Drive or walk along the waterfront for picturesque photo opportunities.

According to legend, British writer John Ruskin once enjoyed tea under the shade of the "Ruskin Oak." Though located on private property, the 350-year-old tree can be viewed from Ruskin Street. The tree is wider than the camera lens.

OCEAN SPRINGS, MISSISSIPPI

Long known as a haven for artists, this quiet harbor town with its shady sidewalks and spreading oak trees rests on the east side of Biloxi Bay. The mineral springs that once offered curative waters to Native Americans and world travelers no longer flow here, but the city calmly restores the souls of visitors. In its picturesque setting, both artists and authors, sometimes one and the same, have found creative inspiration. A legendary visit from one European writer-artist and one Mississippi artist-writer make Ocean Springs a worthy stop for the literary traveler, as well as a home for some contemporary authors.

Long before Walter Inglis Anderson gained fame for *The Horn Island Logs* and his paintings, locals were spinning a tale about British watercolorist and writer John Ruskin (1819-1900). Legend has it that in 1885 Ruskin attended the Cotton Exposition in New Orleans and traveled to Ocean Springs to visit his English friend John B. Arnold, president of the Cotton Exchange in New Orleans and owner of a beachside cottage in Ocean Springs. Sitting under a 350-year-old majestic Live Oak, the Arnold family and Ruskin enjoyed an English tea. Of course, there's no evidence Ruskin ever visited America much less Ocean Springs, but as a naturalist, he would have appreciated the tree now named in his honor. The Ruskin Oak measures more than twenty-eight feet in circumference and stands in the residential neighborhood, Ruskin Oaks.

To see the Ruskin Oak, from the center of downtown **take Porter Ave., go west to Saint John's Episcopal Church on the corner of Porter and Rayburn. Take a left on Rayburn and go one block to Cleveland, then take a right one block to Ruskin St. The oak is at the end of Ruskin on the right (westside).**

Walter Inglis Anderson (1903-1965), most famous for his watercolors and illustrations, wrote more than ninety journals and logbooks. He has been compared to Henry David Thoreau, John Muir, and Aldo Leopold. His most noted work as a writer is *The Horn Island Logs*, published posthumously. A prolific writer, only about a fourth of his writing has been released. He also wrote books describing his bicycle travels in New York City, New Orleans, Texas, Florida, China, and Costa Rica. Along with these works, he left essays, fairy tales, short stories, an illustrated alphabet book, and poetry.

A native of New Orleans, Anderson moved to Ocean Springs after studying at prestigious northern art schools. In Ocean Springs, he worked with the family business, **Shearwater Pottery (102 Shearwater Dr.)**. The last twenty years of his life, he wrote *The Horn Island Logs*, a record of his life, experiences,

Shearwater Pottery at 102 Shearwater Drive in Ocean Springs, still owned and operated by the Anderson family, has a small museum and a shop selling handmade pottery and books about and by Walter Anderson, Mississippi's most famous artist.

and observations of nature on Horn Island, the largest of four barrier islands off the Mississippi coast. Anderson would row or sail the eight miles to the island wilderness to paint, write, and study nature. He'd often spend days at a time observing the island's creatures — crabs, insects, birds — at times seeking shelter from storms by beaching and overturning his boat and climbing underneath. In town, he painted primarily in a family cottage he had inherited. There, he painted the walls and ceiling and created "The Little Room," his personal artistic space. The Little Room and his boat are on display, along with his work, that of his brothers, and traveling exhibits at the Walter Anderson Museum of Art. His murals depicting the history of the area are on the walls in the adjoining community center at **510 Washington Ave., in Ocean Springs.**

The painted room from Walter Anderson's art studio was the inspiration for *Smack Dab in the Middle of Maybe,* a young adult novel by Jo Hackl. The room has been reassembled in the Walter Anderson Museum of Art in Ocean Springs.

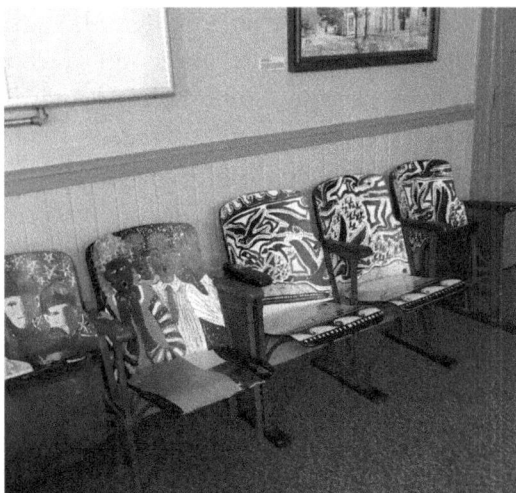

Walter Anderson's presence is everywhere in the artsy town of Ocean Springs. Old auditorium seats in the Mary C. O'Keefe Cultural Arts Center feature designs reminiscent of Walter Anderson's style. Upstairs, aspiring artists take classes.

Horn Island is part of the Gulf Islands National Seashore and accessible only by private boat. It is a designated wilderness area, but private tours are available with authorized commercial operators listed on the National Park Service website or at the **Gulf Islands National Seashore** office at **3500 Park Rd., Ocean Springs.**

Walter Anderson's life and work inspired author Jo Watson Hackl when she wrote her debut novel, *Smack Dab in the Middle of Maybe.* The middle-grade book was awarded the Southern Book Prize in 2019 and is a *Publishers' Weekly* bestseller. Hackl was born in Biloxi at Keesler Air Force Base, and, until she was eleven, lived in Biloxi, just across the bay from Ocean Springs. She used the life of her favorite artist, Walter Anderson, and his painted "Little Room" as key elements in the plot of *Smack Dab in the Middle of Maybe.* In the coming-of-age novel, twelve-year-old protagonist Cricket learns to survive in the wilderness as she follows a mysterious trail of clues leading to the "The Bird Room." The book is an enjoyable reading adventure for adults as well as young adults. Hackl now lives in Greenville, South Carolina.

National Book Award winner Ellen Gilchrist (1935-2024), also a Mississippi native, used "Ocean Springs" as the title for an early short story. In 2017, she was working on a mystery novella featuring a fictional Ocean Springs female detective. For decades, Gilchrist spent her summers at her home in Ocean Springs to be with family, especially grandchildren and great-grandchildren. The rest of the year, she lived in Fayetteville, Arkansas, where she taught at the University of Arkansas. She won the National Book Award in 1984 for a collection of short stories and is also known for her poetry and novels. Gilchrist wrote more than a dozen collections of short stories.

Artist and environmentalist Walter Inglis Anderson lived at Oldfields, a historic Gautier property now belonging to the State of Mississippi. The home, which survived Hurricane Katrina, overlooks the Mississippi Sound.

GAUTIER, MISSISSIPPI

Pronounced GO-shay, this town located between the larger towns of Ocean Springs and Pascagoula, offers breathtaking views of the Mississippi Sound, the Pascagoula River, bayous, and marshes. The town's name originates from Fernando Gautier, who founded a sawmill along the river in 1867. Exponential growth followed Gautier's incorporation more than a hundred years later in 1986.

Walter Inglis Anderson, when recuperating from hospitalization for mental illness, lived with his wife and children in Gautier at the antebellum home Oldfields. The home, originally a pecan plantation which belonged to his wife's family, sits high on a bluff overlooking the Mississippi Sound and Horn Island. Here, freed from the family pottery business, Anderson was able to write and entertain his children with art and stories. Severely damaged in Hurricane Katrina, remarkably, the house still stands at **1901 Water's Edge Dr., in Gautier.** His wife, Agnes Grinstead Anderson (1909-1991), and his daughter Leif Anderson (1944-) also lived in the house and have both written books about Walter Anderson. Now known as the Lewis-Oldfields House, the

Oldfields, the family home of Walter Inglis Anderson's wife Agnes Grinstead, offers a view across the Mississippi Sound from the backyard. When living here with his family, Anderson would row twelve miles across the Sound to Horn Island, where he recorded his observations in what would become *The Horn Island Logs of Walter Inglis Anderson.*

home is on the state's 10 Most Endangered Historic Places list. A visionary environmentalist, in 1944 Anderson recorded log entries describing a walking tour north of Gautier to a colony of sandhill cranes. In 1975, ten years after Anderson's death, the U.S. Fish and Wildlife Service established the Mississippi Sandhill Crane National Wildlife Refuge for the endangered Mississippi Sandhill Crane and its disappearing wet pine savanna habitat. Only about a hundred of the cranes are still in existence, and the bird is considered the rarest in America. Guided tours of the wildlife refuge are available at the **Mississippi Sandhill Crane National Wildlife Refuge at 7200 Crane Ln., Gautier.** Anderson's painting of the sandhill cranes at dawn adorns a portion of the east wall in the artist's Little Room, now in the Walter Anderson Museum of Art. (See Ocean Springs, MS)

While most of Mississippi native Carolyn Haines' bestselling cozy mysteries are set in the Mississippi Delta, a more serious mystery, *Judas Burning*, is set in southeast Mississippi and includes references to both Gautier and Pascagoula. The book features a fictional town, Jexville, and tragedy on a sandbar in the Pascagoula River. In another of her books, *Revenant*, the main character, a journalist, lives in Ocean Springs. Haines grew up in nearby Lucedale, Mississippi, and teaches creative writing at the University of South Alabama. (See Biloxi, MS and Mobile, AL)

PASCAGOULA, MISSISSIPPI

The sleepy little town of Pascagoula, as songwriter Ray Stevens describes it in his comic song "Mississippi Squirrel Revival," rests 100 miles east of New Orleans and 60 miles west of Mobile along the Mississippi Sound. Pascagoula, its coastal waters, and its river have inspired legends, crusaders, and romantics since as early as the sixteenth century.

Entering the area from either the east or the west, travelers cross the Pascagoula River. In 1539, a legendary priest from Hernando DeSoto's expedition visited the Pascagoula Native American tribe. This legendary white man with a cross brought back the story of the mysterious music made by a mermaid rising out of the Pascagoula waters. Known to many as the Singing River, the waterway does emit a mysterious humming sound. (I know, I've heard it).The most popular legend is that of the Pascagoula tribe walking to its death after their chief fell in love with a princess of the rival Biloxi tribe. Rather than be slaves to the Biloxi, the Pascagoula committed suicide by walking into the river, singing their death knell, taking the Biloxi princess along with them. Locals claim Johnny Preston's 1959 hit song "Running Bear Little White Dove" was inspired by this legend of the Singing River. But like other tales of the river, there's no proof. The song was written by J. P. "The Big Bopper" Richardson who died in the Buddy Holly plane crash, the same year the song made the charts, so no one will ever know if the song is about the Indian lovers of the Pascagoula River.

American poet Henry Wadsworth Longfellow, however, is the source of Pascagoula's most famous legend. Some Pascagoulians believe Longfellow, most remembered for his poems "Hiawatha," "Evangeline," and "Paul Revere's Ride," wrote the poem "The Building of the Ship" while staying at a beach front home in Pascagoula. Nearly 100 years later, the poem gained popularity when FDR copied a five-line stanza and sent it to Winston Churchill in 1941. Churchill hung those "the ship of state" lines in his Chartwell home. The line that gives credence to the Pascagoula legend is "From Pascagoula's sunny bay." Though many would like to think Longfellow stayed in the house overlooking Pascagoula's beach when he penned the poem, there's no evidence. The antebellum mansion, known initially as Bellvue, wasn't built until 1850, a year after the first draft of the poem.

Even though Pascagoula has a long tradition in shipbuilding, Longfellow, too, came from a shipbuilding town, Portland, Maine. The Pascagoula line probably refers to the acquisition of materials from Pascagoula, not the

Though only legend puts Henry Wadsworth Longfellow in Pascagoula, this now-private residence lived a glorious life as The Longfellow House, a private club and resort owned by Ingalls Shipbuilding. Locals like to tell of Longfellow writing his poem "The Building of the Ship" while visiting Pascagoula, but there's no evidence.

shipyard. But the legend was energized after 1938. According to The Historical Marker Project, when Bob Ingalls started Ingalls Shipbuilding in Pascagoula, he needed an upscale place for visiting dignitaries to stay. He purchased the old plantation and changed the name to Longfellow House to reflect the legend. By the 1960s the Longfellow House included a country club, restaurant, cabanas, pool, and a golf course. The home still stands and is once again a private residence at **3401 Beach Blvd.** A historical marker has been erected along the beach, across the street from the house.

Though Tennessee Williams (1911-1983) may never have visited Pascagoula, he set his last full-length play, *A House Not Meant to Stand*, in a fictional crumbling, haunted house in Pascagoula. The Southern Gothic two-act work is an expansion of his earlier one-act, *Some Problems for the Moose Lodge*, also set in Pascagoula. The longer version mentions **Pascagoula High School (now Bayside Village Senior Apartments) at 2903 Pascagoula St.**, and the **Pascagoula Ice House** (only the Mission Revival offices remain) at **3708 Pascagoula St.** When built, both locations were noted for their architecture. Williams' marker on the Mississippi Writers Trail is in Clarksdale.

William Faulkner spent the summers of 1925, 1926, and 1927 along the

Tennessee Williams' play *A House Not Meant to Stand* is set in Pascagoula and includes reference to the Pascagoula Ice House on Pascagoula St., visible from Highway 90. Parts of the once modern facility are still standing, though perhaps not for long.

quiet beach stretch at **1305 Beach Blvd.** Here, sitting under a sprawling oak with his manual typewriter, he wrote *Mosquitoes* and *Wild Palms*. Here too, he fell in love with a local girl Helen Baird, to whom he dedicated both works. When she married someone else in 1927, he presented her with a handwritten book of poems, *Helen: A Courtship and Mississippi Poems*. While in Pascagoula, Faulkner stayed at a beachfront cottage owned by Frank Lewis, an in-law of Paul Stone, who Faulkner knew from Oxford, MS. When Faulkner married Estelle Oldham in 1929, the couple honeymooned in Pascagoula. He visited again in 1955 after having won a Nobel for Literature, the same year he would also win a Pulitzer. A historical marker located on **Beach Blvd., west of Buena Vista St.**, marks the site of the cottage. The oak tree under which Faulkner wrote still stands.

On this same Beach Blvd. in 1954, crusading newspaper publisher and editor Ira B. Harkey (1918-2006) watched a six-foot Ku Klux Klan cross erupt into flames in the yard of his home that backed up to **2203 Beach Blvd.** The residence, with a postal address of **1445 Washington Ave.**, was a brick and glass contemporary structure overlooking the beach. Harkey, who owned and edited the *Pascagoula Chronicle* from 1948 to 1963, used the

On August 29, 2005, the homes of three well-known authors met their fate when Hurricane Katrina ravaged the Mississippi Gulf Coast.

3. Gone with the Wind . . . and RAIN

The Pascagoula residence of Ira Harkey, a Pulitzer Prize winning writer and crusading newspaper editor, made history two times: the Ku Klux Klan burned a cross on the lawn and the book *The South Builds: New Architecture in the Old South* featured the house for its contemporary architecture. The house was located between two streets, and Ira Harkey preferred the more modest address on 1445 Washington Ave. The telephone book, however, listed the address as 1445 Beach Blvd. (now renumbered as 2203 Beach Blvd.). Beach Boulevard overlooks the Mississippi Sound. The modern house was built on steel support columns, with impressive wall-sized glass windows, some covered by crossed steel tension rods, and brick "end caps." The home was built on a slope, and like a split level, had staggered levels: ground, middle and upper. Guests entered on the middle floor into the living room, dining room, and kitchen and breakfast area. For this large family with six children, boys' bedrooms and a game room were on the ground level, leading into an outside play court. Girls' bedrooms, a study and the master bedroom were on the upper level. After the Harkeys left Pascagoula in the1960s, new owners, a facelift, and fully grown landscaping softened the house's stark appearance. The Harkey house weathered the Ku Klux Klan, Hurricane Camille, and Hurricane Frederic. Hurricane Katrina finally brought her down, but several of the Harkey children returned to the Pascagoula area to raise their own families and contribute to the community.

PHOTO COURTESY CITY OF PASCAGOULA

newspaper to crusade for civil rights. He won a Pulitzer Prize in 1963 for a series of editorials on integration and the defense of James Meredith, the first African American to attend the University of Mississippi (Ole Miss). Twice the newspaper's office, located at **310 Delmas Ave.,** suffered broken windows from shotgun and rifle blasts. Personally threatened, Harkey started carrying a handgun. He left Pascagoula in 1963 and went on to earn a Master's and Ph.D., and lecture at colleges and universities. He wrote six books including *The Smell of Burning Crosses*, which covers the incidents in Pascagoula. In 1993, he was admitted to the Mississippi Press Association's Hall of Fame. The residence, which is featured in the book *The South Builds: New Architecture in the Old South*, was destroyed by Hurricane Katrina.

The single writer who has made Pascagoula a household name is native-son Jimmy Buffett (1947-2023). One of only six authors to have a *New York Times* bestseller in both fiction (*Where is Joe Merchant?)* and nonfiction (*A Pirate Looks at Fifty*) at the same time, Buffett is best known as a singer and songwriter.

Pascagoulians love Jimmy Buffett. They've given him the key to the city and named a bridge and a part of the beach after him. Highway 90 has a commemorative plaque honoring the town as his birthplace, while a city biking tour includes a stop and marker at his first home on the corner of **Garfield** and **Roosevelt. Buffett Bridge** is located on **Beach Blvd. between Market St. and 11th Ave. and crosses Baptiste Bayou,** where Buffett spent his summers crabbing off his grandfather's pier on **Parsley Ave**. The small bridge is adorned with coastal murals painted by local artist Brenda Kitchens. The town's name and his Uncle Billy Buffett, who lived there, inspired the hit "Pascagoula Run." Along with songs, fiction and nonfiction, Buffett wrote children's books with daughter Savannah Jane Buffett.

Before Jimmy Buffett's 1989 release of "Pascagoula Run," the city earned headlines worldwide with the most documented case ever of an alien encounter when Charles Hickson and Calvin Parker were allegedly abducted while night fishing on the Pascagoula River in 1973. The City of Pascagoula has commemorated the abduction with a marker at **Lighthouse Park (3621 Frederic St. near Hwy. 90)** on the east side of the river under the Pascagoula River Bridge. The marker is not too far from the abduction site Parker writes about in his books, *Pascagoula – The Closest Encounter: My Story* (2018) and *Pascagoula: The Story Continues – New Evidence and New Witnesses* (2019). The books, published by Flying Disc Press in West Yorkshire, England, are printed in several languages. The eBook was a bestseller. Author Calvin Parker lives about five miles from the abduction site in Moss Point.

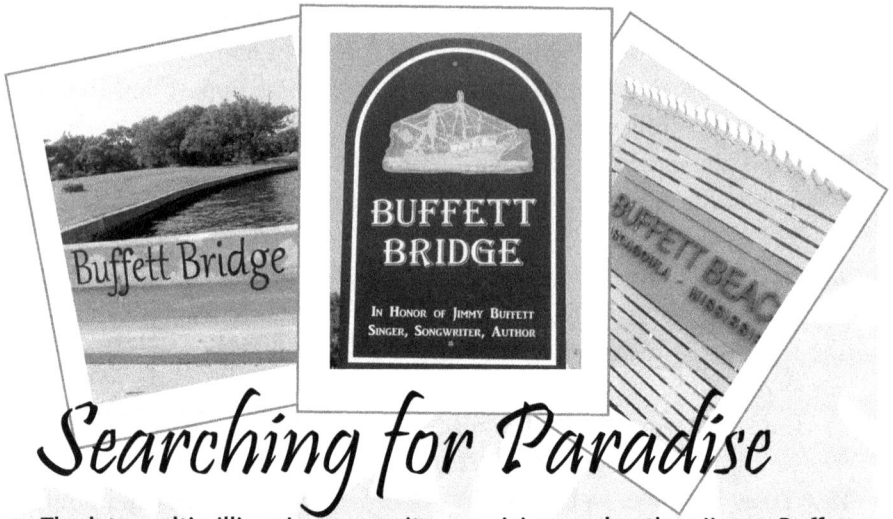

BUFFETT
BRIDGE

IN HONOR OF JIMMY BUFFETT
SINGER, SONGWRITER, AUTHOR

Searching for Paradise

The late multimillionaire songwriter, musician, and author Jimmy Buffett has Parrot Head fans from coast to coast who follow his music, concerts, and lifestyle dressed in parrot head hats, flashing "fins up" head salutes, and wearing tropical attire (even grass skirts and coconut bras). The worldwide official Jimmy Buffett fan club, Parrot Heads in Paradise Foundation, has donated more than $58 million and 4.5 million volunteer hours for charities since its origin in 2002, according to the PHIP website. Buffett's private foundation, Singing for Change, redistributes one dollar for every concert ticket sold into community grants, well over $11 million awarded so far.

Along with popularity, Buffett has garnered bestseller accolades and gold and platinum record albums. Born in Pascagoula and raised in Mobile, he is endeared to the hearts of locals for more than being a native son. When the BP Oil Spill of 2010 marred the Gulf and shattered the tourism trade, Buffett organized a beach benefit concert in Gulf Shores to raise the spirits of thousands and draw attention nationwide to the tragedy. That same summer he opened his Margaritaville Hotel on Pensacola Beach, despite the disaster, dismal tourist trade, and closed beaches. He loved the area, and the area still loves him back. Locals tell of hearing a familiar voice and a few guitar chords, and following the music to find Jimmy Buffett playing in a local club, the Land Shark beach bar or his sister's place – unannounced – just dropping in to sing.

Tune into some music and drive past these Jimmy Buffett sights.

JIMMY BUFFETT TRAIL

BILOXI (MS) – Margaritaville Hotel & Resort
GAUTIER (MS) – Childhood Easter Egg hunts at aunt and
   uncle's house south of Creosote Plant off Graveline Rd.
PASCAGOULA (MS) – Birthplace
   First home at intersection Garfield and Roosevelt
   Buffett Bridge near favorite fishing spot on Beach Blvd.
   Grandfather's bayou near Parsley Ave.
MOBILE (AL) – Hometown
   St. Ignatius Catholic School – grade school
   McGill-Toolen Catholic High School – high school
   St. Joseph's Chapel at Spring Hill College – first wedding
   Admiral's Corner at the Admiral Hotel - 251 Government
      St., performed here in early days
   Product Sound Studio - cut first record (studio destroyed
      by a tornado on his birthday 2012) 1916 Airport Blvd.
   Dew Drop Inn – legendary inspiraton for "Cheeseburger in
      Paradise," 1808 Old Shell Rd.
DAUPHIN ISLAND
   Love of history fueled by climbing around Fort Morgan
      as a kid
FAIRHOPE (AL)
   Parents lived here, he lived here, parents buried here
GULF SHORES (AL)
   Surfed here in a hurricane
   Hung out at Hangout as a student
   Sister Lucy Buffett's restaurant, LuLu's
   Site of BP Oil Spill benefit beach concert
PENSACOLA BEACH (FL)
   First Margaritaville Hotel (now Pensacola Beach Resort)
      and the beach where he enjoyed the sunsets in the fall
      and learned to surf in shallow waves in the summer
PANAMA CITY BEACH (FL)
   Searched for surf as a teenager

Lower Alabama

Alabama

Alabama's rich literary tradition includes household names like Harper Lee, author of *To Kill A Mockingbird*, and Forrest Gump, the main character of Winston Groom's novel of the same name. The state is also noted for its annual Shakespeare festival, one of the ten largest in the world, bringing more than 300,000 visitors, playwrights, actors, and scholars to Montgomery every year. The performances are held in an indoor re-creation of Shakespeare's Globe Theatre. Despite Shakespeare's Globe, Harper Lee's hometown of Monroeville is considered the Literary Capital of Alabama. The city hosts an annual literary festival featuring prose, poetry, spoken word, and music. And, of course, tours of the famous courthouse from *To Kill A Mockingbird*.

Alabama Coastal Community College in Monroeville is home to the Alabama Center for Literary Arts and sponsors an annual symposium. Portraits of the state's literary icons are on display at the Alabama Writers' Hall of Honor.

The state's Pulitzer Prize winners for literature include Harper Lee, Winston Groom, T.S. Stribling, and Shirley Ann Grau. Those winning Pulitzer Prizes for nonfiction include journalists Rick Bragg, Cynthia Tucker, Howell Raines and Harold E. Martin, and biologist Edward O. Wilson.

The Alabama Writers' Forum, in conjunction with the Alabama Center for the Book, honors outstanding Alabama writers by inducting them into the Alabama Writers Hall of Fame. AWF also fosters literary arts in the community and schools, keeps an up-to-date online Contemporary Writers Directory, and sponsors the Harper Lee Award, honoring a writer born in Alabama or whose formative work was written while in the state. An impressive number of these honorees still live in Alabama.

The Alabama Writers Conclave names a poet laureate every four years and holds an annual conference and yearly writing contests.

As part of the tri-state Southern Literary Trail, Alabama showcases writer's homes and museums, statues, parks, and buildings honoring authors. While Mobile is listed on the Southern Literary Trail, Lower Alabama, that portion of the state stretching from Mobile south and eastward to the Florida line, also deserves recognition. Several honorees of the Alabama Writers Hall of Fame call the area home. Some claim more writers live here than in any other place in the country. Writers are invited, encouraged, and appreciated in Lower Alabama — affectionately known as LA — a place rich in unique settings and memorable characters.

MOBILE, ALABAMA

Founded in 1702, Mobile boasts Alabama's first literary figure, André Penigaut (1638-?) who wrote of the French exploration of Mobile Bay in *Annals of Louisiana from 1698 to 1722*. These journals, published posthumously, provide a twenty-year account of the settlement of the Gulf South.

Naturalist and author William Bartram (1739–1823) of Pennsylvania visited the Mobile area in 1775, in particular Fort Condé (visitors can see a replica of the colonial fort adjacent to the **History Museum of Mobile, 150 South Royal St.**). His observations are recorded in a book now considered by some as the first environmentalist book. Though most readers call the book *Bartram's Travels*, the very descriptive, official title of the tome is *Travels Through North and South Carolina, Georgia, East and West Florida, the Cherokee Country, the Extensive Territories of the Muscogulges or Creek Confederacy, and the Country of the Chactaws. Containing an Account of the Soil and Natural Productions of Those Regions; Together with Observations on the Manners of the Indians.*

No wonder folks call it *Bartram's Travels*.

Almost every historical era to the present lists unique literary figures writing and living in Mobile. Women writers, in increasing numbers, have brought notice to the city's literary scene, especially at times when few females were published authors. Still today, a strong cadre of female writers calls Mobile home. When the **History Museum of Mobile (111 South Royal St.)** created its 2021 exhibit, "A History of Mobile in 22 Objects," a selection of "unexpected objects" told the 300-year history of the city. The city's appreciation and value of literature is evident as two of the twenty-two objects represent the written word. Object 18, the typewriter on which John LeFlore wrote more than 50,000 letters in his crusade, represents the battle for civil rights justice. The "Mobile Bookshelf," Object 20, includes books by Eugene Walter, Winston Groom, and N. K. Jemisin. The accompanying placard explains the rich literary tradition of the city dating to the 1800s.

Augusta Jane Evans or Augusta Evans Wilson (1835–1909) is documented as the first woman to earn $100,000 (U.S.) through her writing and as Alabama's first professional writer (based on book sales). At age fifteen, after her family arrived in Mobile from Texas, she wrote her first book, *Inez: A Tale of the Alamo*, surprisingly now available online. With the proceeds from the book, she bought her father a home which still stands. **Georgia Cottage (The Augusta Evans Wilson Home) is located at 2564 Spring Hill Ave.**

SAINTLY CITIES

St. Elmo, the 1866 novel by Augusta Evans Wilson, was wildly popular across the country. In its first four months of publication, the book sold over a million copies. Items like cigars, steamboats, and punch were named for St. Elmo, the novel's evil character who turns his life around. Even newly formed communities named themselves St. Elmo.

St. Elmo, **ALABAMA**, is an unincorporated city in Mobile County with its own St. Elmo Fire Department, but it's not the historic St. Elmo Fire Hall • St. Elmo in **TENNESSEE** is a Chatanooga neighborhood and historic district named for the book and where the author finished the book. It's also the site of St. Elmo Fire Hall, a restored 1930s firestation, now a popular event venue, appropriately located on St. Elmo Avenue • St. Elmo, **ILLINOIS**, is where steamships were built • **COLORADO**'s St. Elmo is both a ghost town and a hotel • **TEXAS** has two St. Elmos. The one in Freestone County is named for the book.

And then there's the fictional St. Elmo and St. Elmo Island in **FLORIDA**, the settings in Michaela Thompson's *Florida Panhandle Mysteries*.

and is on the National Register of Historic Places. Still a private residence, a historic marker is visible from the street next to the driveway. *St. Elmo*, her most popular novel, was turned into a silent film in 1914 and again in 1923, but both are now considered lost. Though the book is not set in the Mobile area, St. Elmo, a small community seven miles southwest of Mobile on Hwy. 90, is named after the book. Another town, closer to the fictional setting of the book near Lookout Mountain, Tennessee, is also named St. Elmo after the novel. Ironically, St. Elmo is a character in the book, not a location.

During the Civil War, Evans nursed sick and wounded Confederate troops at **Fort Morgan** (on Mobile Point at the tip of the peninsula west of Gulf Shores). It must have been seemed wild and isolated at the time, considering it's still fairly primitive today, especially if you arrive by the **Mobile Bay Ferry** from Dauphin Island **(State Hwy. 193 from Mobile to 112 Bienville Dr.)** In Mobile, Evans set up a hospital near her home. Locals dubbed it "Camp Beulah," a play on words after the title of her 1859 novel *Beulah*. When she married, she moved to her husband's estate, Ashland House, and wrote three novels there. Though the antebellum home burned down in 1926, the **Ashland Place Historic District** evokes a feel for history. The district is bordered by **Spring Hill Ave., Ryan Ave., LeVert Ave., and Old Shell Rd.** She is buried at **Magnolia Cemetery, 1202 Virginia St.**

COME TO THE MARDI GRAS!

Mobile, Alabama, is the mother of all Mardi Gras – literally. All along the stretch from Bay St. Louis to Apalachicola, you'll experience the flavor of Mardi Gras at least two months out of the year. Day and night parades, feeds, carnival balls, and hometown revelry fill the social calendars. Each town does it differently, and each town boasts a signature event. Here's a sampling.

Bay St. Louis (MS)
• Scores of children from Krewe of Kids decorate nonmotorized vehicles and don costumes to parade through a park, with the merriment culminating at an assisted living facility.

Biloxi (MS)
• Mardi Gras season opens every Jan. 5 with a Twelfth Night celebration. The Biloxi Lighthouse goes "dark" and the Mardi Gras Museum is illuminated, and, of course, there's a parade.

Gautier (MS)
• Gautier Men's Club and local authorities stop traffic for this lighted night parade as it rolls down U.S. Hwy. 90.

Mobile (AL)
• Joe Cain Day celebrates the founder of Mardi Gras. The Sunday before Mardi Gras (Fat Tuesday), festivities begin at Joe Cain's gravesite and revelers in mourning follow his Merry Widows to the craziest parade of the season. Yep, he was a real guy.

Gulf Shores (AL)
• Costumed revelers (and diners) enjoy live music and watch a daytime boat parade cruise along the Intracoastal Waterway every year at Lucy Buffett's LuLu's restaurant. Rather than King Cake, LuLu's serves free birthday-anniversary cake.

Pensacola Beach (FL)
• Krewe of Wrecks ladles out Red Beans & Rice on Pensacola Beach. Free food cooked in giant pots is served under a tent by bead-wearing members of the carnival krewe.

Fort Walton Beach (FL)
•The Krewe of Bowlegs, a swashbuckling bunch of pirates and wenches with a pirate ship, parade all year and are a favorite at Mardi Gras parades. They sponsor a June pirate festival. Yep, Billy Bowlegs was a real Seminole chief.

Ashland Place, a 40-acre Mobile historic district with about 80 homes, is listed on the National Register of Historic Places. The neighborhood occupies the land of the estate of the first successful female novelist, Augusta Evans Wilson. The original entry gates and archway shown above marked Wilson's home, built around 1900.

A portion of **Augusta St.** named after Augusta Evans Wilson passes through the **Oakleigh Garden Historic District,** a quaint residential area with homes dating as far back as 1820. A focal point is **Washington Square**. The former **home of Joe Cain,** patron saint of Mobile Mardi Gras, is located at **906 Augusta St.** An Alabama Bicentennial marker commemorates the site.

Ashland Place Historic District pays homage to Mobile literati with all four streets named after writers — LeVert, Ryan, DeLeon, and Lanier. The first three are often known by their unique epithets: Thomas Coooper DeLeon, Blind Laureate of the Lost Cause; Octavia Walton LeVert, The Pride of Mobile; and Father Abram Ryan, the Poet-Priest of the Confederacy. The fourth honoree, Sidney Lanier, spent a winter at Point Clear on Mobile Bay for health reasons.

Travelers not interested in literary street names will still enjoy the enchanting ride through Ashland Place viewing its gorgeous homes creating one of Mobile's finest neighborhoods. The 81-home neighborhood, built in the 1920s and 1930s, stands on the property of Augusta Jane Evans' former 40-acre estate which burned. It seems only fitting the streets in a neighborhood where the first successful woman writer penned three novels are named after famous writers. The entrance arch, two stucco guard houses, and pedestals on each side of the arch are the remnants of the entrance to Augusta Evans' grand estate. They are still grand today.

The streets and the writers they are named for begin with Thomas Cooper DeLeon (1839-1914), a poet, editor, journalist, novelist, and playwright who lived in Mobile the last thirty years of his life. He edited several newspapers including the *Mobile Register*. His most noted work is *Belles, Beaux and Brains of the Sixties*, published in 1909. The book contains profiles of notable individuals ranging from socialites, politicians and military figures to writers and artists living in the era before and after the Civil War. One chapter includes mention of Madame Octavia LeVert's literary salon in Mobile. The book also includes portraits, some rare, of the historical figures. DeLeon is buried in **Magnolia Cemetery at 1202 Virginia St.**

Octavia Walton LeVert, as a young socialite visiting Baltimore in 1827, was the object of the poem "To Octavia" by Edgar Allan Poe. Scholars question whether Poe wrote the poem for her or simply inscribed the nine lines in Octavia's album. After she moved to Mobile and married Dr. LeVert, she acquired the respected title Madame LeVert and entertained hundreds of people — all were welcome — at her Monday salons, reflective of the popular literary salons of Europe. The home where she entertained at the intersection of **Royal St. and Government St.** was demolished in the mid-1900s and replaced with a courthouse. However, **Dr. LeVert's office at 153 Government St.,** complete with historical plaque, is the headquarters of the Mobile Bar Association. The building served as a doctor's office for a hundred years.

Following the Civil War, Father Abram Joseph Ryan (1838-1886), the Catholic priest dubbed the "Poet-Priest of the Confederacy," spent ten years in Mobile. He was first assigned as an assistant at **Cathedral Basilica of the Immaculate Conception (2 South Claiborne St.)** and then as pastor at **St. Mary's (1453 Old Shell Rd.).** His presence is honored in Mobile with a bust and a portrait in an upstairs study where he once lived at **Portier House (307 Conti St.)** and at **Father Ryan Memorial Park (700-800 Spring Hill Ave.)** in downtown with a bronze six-foot statue of him holding a book of poetry. The park was the site of protests in 2017 and 2020 calling for the removal of Confederate statues. Though the priest did not die in Mobile, he loved the city so much he requested his body be returned to St. Mary's and buried there. His grave is in **Old Catholic Cemetery, 1700 Martin Luther King Dr.** (See Biloxi, MS)

Lanier Street is named for Sidney Lanier, noted poet of the mid and

A statue of Father Abram Ryan, the Poet-Priest of the Confederacy, is the centerpiece of Father Ryan Memorial Park on Springhill Avenue in Mobile. The likeness of Ryan holds a book of poetry.

late 1800s who lived in Point Clear across Mobile Bay while recuperating from illness. He also lived in Montgomery and Prattville, Alabama, where he taught. His most noted poems include "Marshes of the Glynn." Generations of school children memorized and recited his poems about nature as recent as the 1960s.

Archibald Gracie IV (1858-1912), a *Titanic* survivor who wrote an account of the sinking of the ship, was born in Mobile, where his father had family interests in the cotton market. His book, *Titanic: A Survivor's Story*, is still in print, and Gracie's character appears in several *Titanic* films.

In 1920, Sherwood Anderson (1876-1941), who had already published *Winesburg, Ohio*, traveled to Mobile to help recover from flu-like symptoms. In the back room of a bootleg joint, he eavesdropped on three drunken sailors and listened to their tales. From that experience he wrote a murder scene for his novel *Poor White*. (See Fairhope, AL)

An author who wrote under two names, Marie Layet Sheip (1885-1936) lived in her birthplace of Mobile after being orphaned until she was sixteen. She was raised by her grandmother who was friends with Augusta Evans Wilson, the popular novelist at the time. Following her grandmother's death, Marie lived with relatives out of state but returned to Mobile at age twenty-four. To support herself, she wrote at least six scripts for silent films.

In 1930, after marrying wealthy lumberman Stanley Sheip, she published the novel *Gulf Stream* under the pseudonym Marie Stanley — a nom de plume combining their names. The book is noteworthy as literary fiction and for its subject matter at the time: interracial relationships and marriage. The novel received national acclaim, but locally caused a disturbance from residents of Sandtown, an African American section of Mobile which was the setting of the book. Residents objected to the use of dialect and portrayal of Black culture by a white author. While other settings in the book had fictional names as Silver Hill for Spring Hill, Sandtown's name was not disguised. Sandtown, established before 1845, is the oldest African American neighborhood in Mobile, and lies within the Spring Hill District.

The book was republished by the University of Alabama press in 1993 with a preface by Mobile historian Caldwell Delaney.

Marie Sheip and husband Stanley lived on a seventeen-acre estate in the Spring Hill section of Mobile in a home they called Wakewood. There they entertained fellow writers the likes of William March.

Marie's parents were residing at the Battle House Hotel at the time of her birth. She died in Apalachicola. (See Apalachicola, FL)

William March was the pen name of bestselling novelist William Edward Campbell (1893-1954), who was born in Mobile and spent most of his childhood and teenage years there. A decorated combat veteran, he suffered from PTSD and wrote as a form of self-therapy. After World War I and living abroad, he moved to New York. When he began suffering depression, his Mobile friends traveled to New York and moved him to **The Grand Hotel in Point Clear, Alabama,** where he may have lived in a suite for eleven months. (The hotel records are missing from this time). Once healthy, he moved to Mobile to the **Battle House Hotel (26 N. Royal St.)**, then rented an apartment on **Government St.**, and later one on **Conti St.**, where he worked on *The Bad Seed*, his most acclaimed work. *The Bad Seed* was made into a film starring child actor Patty McCormick. Winner of four O. Henry Awards for his short stories and author of several novels, Campbell set much of his work in Alabama. His mother's maiden name was March, the origin of his pseudonym. (See Point Clear, AL)

Doris Jean Austin (1949-1994), an African American journalist, novelist and short story writer, was born in Mobile and lived there until she was six. Her critically acclaimed and only novel, *After the Garden*, traces a young Black woman's life in Jersey City from the 1940s to the 1960s. Austin's lifelong friend, bestselling author Terry McMillan, patterned the character Delilah in *How Stella Got Her Groove Back* on Austin.

Bestseller author, songwriter, and musician Jimmy Buffett (1946-2023) attended what is now **McGill-Toolen High School (1501 Old Shell Rd.)** and was married at **St. Joseph's Chapel** on the campus of **Spring Hill College**. Before making the big time, he often performed at the **Admiral's Corner at the Admiral Hotel (251 Government St.)** He cut his first record at **Product Sound Studio** above a dentist's office, which stood at **1916 Airport Blvd.** The building was destroyed on Buffetts' birthday in the Christmas Day Tornado of 2013. (See Fairhope, AL and Pascagoula, MS)

A bevy of well-read contemporary women authors also call Mobile and its surrounds home. Award-winning, bestselling author Carolyn Haines, who writes under the pen names R.B. Chesterton, Caroline Burnes, and Lizzie Hart, lives in nearby Semmes. She has written more than eighty cozy mysteries, historical mysteries, and romance novels. Inducted into the Alabama Writers Hall of Fame in 2020, she is also a recipient of a Harper Lee Award as Alabama's Distinguished Writer of the Year and the Richard Wright Award for Literary Excellence. (See Biloxi, MS and Gautier, MS)

USA Today bestselling author Angela Quarles, who writes paranormal romance, contemporary time travel, and steampunk books, owns the **Haunted Book Shop at 109 Dauphin St**. in downtown Mobile. Quarles (whose real name is Angela Trigg) has published nine novels and won a Romance Writers of America RITA award in 2016. After her grandmother died, Angela, a native of Florida, moved into her grandmother's Victorian home at **2000 Dauphin St.** She's the fifth generation to occupy the home, which is nicknamed Termite Hall.

Mobile writer Eugene Walter titled his 1982 cookbook *Delectable Dishes from Termite Hall* after the home, which was a literary hub of notable writers. The family resident at the time was Adelaide Trigg, Angela's grandmother, and co-owner of the first Haunted Book Shop in Mobile. Termite Hall, officially listed as the **Greene-Marston House,** is on the National Register

Built in 1833 as a family sanctuary from the subtropical climate of Mobile and the yellow fever epidemic, Historic Oakleigh House inspired the *Seven Sisters* novels of Mobile writer M. L. Bullock. The home is located at 300 Oakleigh Place in the Oakleigh Garden Historic District. The tour is well worth the ticket price.

of Historic Places and located at **2000 Dauphin St.**

A visit to the **Historic Oakleigh House Museum at 300 Oakleigh Pl.** in Mobile's **Oakleigh Garden Historic District** inspired M. L. Bullock (Monica Leigh Bullock) to write her first novel, *Seven Sisters*, the beginning of a series of supernatural suspense books. The Queen of Southern Gothic, she's since sold more than nine million books. Her *Seven Sisters* series is set in Mobile. The first book pays homage to historic homes in Mobile as the main character, a historian who dreams of the past, inventories and refits an antebellum home during its restoration. The author also pays homage to Mobile's first writer of acclaim, Augusta Evans, with several mentions in the cozy paranormal-romantic mystery. Bullock lives in coastal Alabama.

Oakleigh's historic collection includes first editions of several of Augusta Evans' romance novels. They're located in the second-story office in the over-sized bookcases. Oil portraits of both Evans' mother and father are also on display on the second floor.

Winding through the Oakleigh Garden Historic District, readers can imagine the houses in which Evans' antebellum characters might have dwelled, with some of the 200-plus houses in the neighborhood dating as far

In 1998, the impressive Cathedral Basilica of the Immaculate Conception on Claiborne Street in downtown Mobile was the site of the funeral of Alabama's Renaissance Man and all-around Southern character, Eugene Walter. When living in Paris, Walter was an early contributor to *The Paris Review*. His funeral was followed by a jazz processional. His gravesite is in historic Church Street Cemetery, on Church St. between Highwy 90 (Broad St.) and South Warren in downtown Mobile.

back as the 1820s.

Eugene Walter (1921-1998), poet, screenwriter, playwright, and short story writer, was dubbed "Mobile's Renaissance Man." After World War II he lived in Paris and helped launch *The Paris Review*. When living in Rome, he translated and acted in films of Federico Fellini. He returned to Mobile in 1979. His first novel, *The Untidy Pilgrim*, won the Lippincott Fiction Prize, but in later years he was best known for cookbooks and magazine articles. When he died, his wake was held at **Scottish Rite Temple at 351 St. Francis St.** and his funeral at historic **Cathedral Basilica of the Immaculate Conception (2 S. Claiborne St.).** The funeral entourage was followed by a jazz processional. Walter was buried in the historic **Church Street Graveyard (805 Church St.)** by special permission; the cemetery no longer buried the dead after the 1890s.

While she was living in Mobile, oral historian, biographer, and novelist Katherine Clark spent four months with the author and actor Eugene Walter. The result is the book *Milking the Moon: A Southerner's Life on This Planet*. (See Pensacola, FL)

BIRDWATCHING

BIRDWATCHER'S PARADISE

Oswald T. Campbell, the main character in Fannie Flagg's *A Redbird Christmas* discovers his passion for birds in Lost River, the fictional version of Magnolia Springs, Alabama. To experience Oswald's wonder, visit Weeks Bay, near Magnolia Springs, or another of these bird paradises. All three states offer birding trails.

MISSISSIPPI

Driving along Highway 90 (Beach Blvd.) between Gulfport and Biloxi in May and June, travelers will see scores of endangered Least Terns nesting – right on the beach within eyesight of swimmers, bikers, tourists, and passing vehicles. These protected areas are home to the largest nesting site of Least Terns in the U.S. and have been named a Globally Important Bird Area.

A critically endangered species, the Mississippi Sandhill Crane has found safe haven at the **Mississippi Sandhill Crane National Wildlife Refuge in Gautier**. This species is considered one of the rarest bird populations on earth; only about 100 of these red-topped cranes exist. The only place in the wild where they can be seen is at this refuge, according to a U.S. Fish & Wildlife Service brochure. Mississippi's Coastal Birding Trail, sponsored by the National Audubon Society, has stops all along the coast, although most are located in the Pascagoula-Gautier area.

The Pascagoula River Audubon Center in Moss Point offers rocking chairs for birdwatchers to sit while they watch. The Pascagoula River habitat, part of the greater Mississippi Flyway migratory stopover, is home to more than 300 species of birds.

ALABAMA

Birdwatchers can follow the U.S. Fish & Wildlife Service's **Alabama Coastal Birding Trail** to experience the six most popular birding trails along the coast. Designed as loops, the trails include wildlife preserves, piers, scenic overlooks, and city, county, state, and federal parks. Along the trail, kiosks offer information and bird lists. Popular spots on the trail are **Weeks Bay, Bon Secour, and Dauphin Island**.

Weeks Bay National Estuarine Research Reserve is home to almost 350 species, many which can be spotted from the observation boardwalk and tower. Millions of birds fly over **Bon Secour National Wildlife Refuge** during migration. Ask for the official U.S. Fish & Wildlife Bird Checklist with 379 species listed.

More than 400 species have been reported from **Dauphin Island**, which is one of the four top migratory birdwatching locations in the U.S. The island is recognized as a Globally Important Bird Area by the National Audubon Society and BirdLife International. For many migratory tropical birds, Dauphin Island offers the first rest stop. **Dauphin Island Audubon Bird Sanctuary** has six walking trails and observation decks.

FLORIDA

The 2000-mile-long **Great Florida Birding and Wildlife Trail** begins at Big Lagoon State Park in Pensacola and includes several Panhandle stops. At Big Lagoon they'll loan you binoculars to explore the elevated boardwalks and trails through woodlands and wetlands. The impressive three-story observation tower damaged by Hurricane Sally reopened in 2023.

Fort Pickens, part of the Gulf Island National Seashore on Pensacola Beach, has more than 280 identified birds in wetlands, marshes, onshore and off. Birders can pick up a checklist at the Discovery Center. During nesting, 15 mph speed limit signs go up and everything slows down to protect the birds.

St. Andrews State Park in Panama City Beach, and nearby **St. Andrews Bird Trail**, and **Oaks by the Bay Park** in Panama City, offer different levels of birding. Beginning birders can follow the city park's Bird Trail which includes a waterfront boardwalk with bird identification placards while Gator Lake at the state park has a heron rookery in the spring.

St. George Island State Park, officially known as Dr. Julius G. Bruce St. George Island State Park, is a birding hotspot near Apalachicola with over 300 species. The park has an observation tower. Maps are available with bird areas labeled.

Left to right: A gull on Pensacola Beach; signs protect nesting birds on Navarre Beach; a feathered hitchhiker catches a ferry ride to Dauphin Island.

Novelist Michael Knight (1969-), a native of Mobile and Director of the Creative Writing Program at the University of Tennessee, features Mobile and the Mobile Bay area in his collection of short stories *Eveningland*, a 2017 Oprah Pick. His novel *The Typist* was named Best Book of 2011 by *The Huffington Post* and *Kansas City Star*. Knight, described as a Southern writer, won the Robert Penn Warren Prize for Excellence in 2013 and the Truman Capote Award for Short Fiction in 2017.

N. K. Jemisin (Nora Keita Jemisin) (1972 -) no longer calls Mobile home, but as the daughter of divorced parents, she grew up living with her mother in Mobile during the school year and her father in New York in the summers. Now a bestselling, award-winning novelist, many of her childhood hours were spent in the Mobile Public Library. The *New York Times* describes Jemisin as "the most celebrated science fiction and fantasy writer of her generation." She is adapting her *Broken Earth* trilogy for film. Jemisin has written more than ten novels, along with short fiction and a graphic novel.

E. O. Wilson (1929-2021), scientist and winner of the Pulitzer Prize for general nonfiction in 1979 and 1991, was born in Alabama and always considered himself a Mobilian. As a boy, he threw a paper route for the *Mobile Press-Register*. He attended both **Barton Academy (504 Government St.)** and **Murphy High School (100 South Carlen St.),** and eventually taught at Harvard. In a 2010 interview with Jocko Potts for *Mobile Bay Magazine*, Wilson said he had a "deep, spiritual attraction to Mobile," and described Mobile as a city with a soul.

Anthill, Wilson's foray into fiction after winning two Pulitzers for nonfiction, was published in 2010. The novel, which hints of Mobile, won the *Chicago Tribune's* Heartland Prize for fiction.

In 2005, Dauphin Island Sea Lab named its newest research vessel the *EO Wilson*. The literary science writing award bestowed by PEN America is also named in his honor.

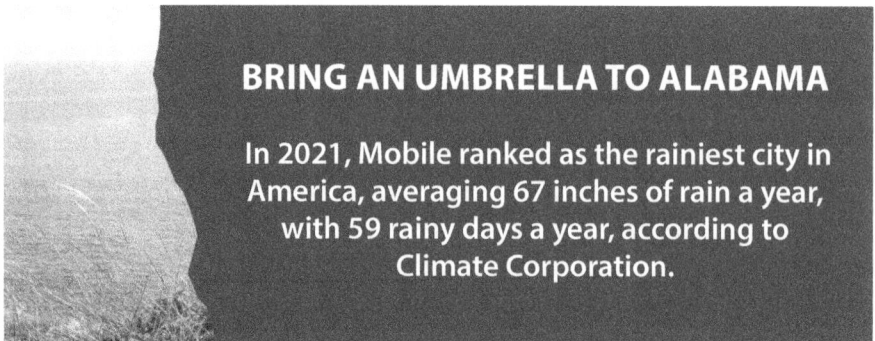

BRING AN UMBRELLA TO ALABAMA

In 2021, Mobile ranked as the rainiest city in America, averaging 67 inches of rain a year, with 59 rainy days a year, according to Climate Corporation.

EASTERN SHORE, ALABAMA

Leaving Mobile, heading east along the "bayway," vehicles still travel on remnants of old Highway 90 near the *Battleship Alabama*. In Jack Kerouac's *On the Road*, the carload of characters travels from Flomaton, Florida, to Mobile, along this stretch of Highway 90. Here, just outside Mobile, the character Dunkel steals three packs of cigarettes from a gas station "without even trying."

Crossing these scenic marshes of Mobile Bay, travelers encounter what locals call the Eastern Shore. The loose geographical term includes cities, towns, and hamlets bordered by Interstate 10 and Highway 31 on the North, State Road 181 on the east, and Highway 98 and Weeks Bay on the south. Included are the larger towns of Fairhope, Daphne, and Spanish Fort, along with smaller ones as Montrose and Point Clear.

Two places south of Eastern Shore, Magnolia Springs and Gulf Shores, offer rich settings for books and retreats for writers. The area inspires authors with its diversity — from the posh 170-year-old Grand Hotel Golf Resort and Spa to the quaint village that still receives its mail by boat along the river.

SPANISH FORT, ALABAMA

This high city on a hill overlooking Mobile Bay looks like suburban sprawl from Mobile. But Spanish Fort has its own rich history and identity. Established in 1712 as a trading post by the French, the Spanish later occupied and built a fort here. The fort was the site of a Civil War battle. Almost a hundred years later, the community experienced population growth and in 1993 was incorporated.

Tom Kelly (1927-), often called the poet laureate of turkey hunting, worked for decades in forest management in his hometown of Mobile before finding his niche in the literary world. He has entertained so many readers with his essays and stories on turkey hunting that before turkey season opens every year, hunters across the South and the entire country read and re-read Kelly's *The Tenth Legion*, his first of more than twenty books.

Before moving to Maryland at age 91 to be close to family, Kelly operated a wild turkey product and marketing company out of Spanish Fort, where he and his wife lived. In 2021, he was still writing several hundred words a day and in 2022, at age 94, the World War II and Korean War veteran harvested a turkey on a hunt in Mississippi.

VISIT THE WILD PLACES

I discovered estuaries reading *V for Victor*, a World War II adventure novel set at Weeks Bay, where the Magnolia River and the Fish River flow into Mobile Bay in Alabama.

I visited Weeks Bay to look for hidden islands, secret inlets, snaking rivers, and German submarines, but discovered the Weeks Bay National Estuarine Research Reserve. That visit sent me on a wild adventure to other wetland wildernesses in Florida and Mississippi.

Mississippi, Alabama, and Florida have each partnered with NOAA (National Oceanic and Atmospheric Administration) and NOS (National Ocean Service) to preserve and protect the wild places where the rivers meet the sea — estuaries, marshes, swamps, bayous, bays, bogs, and all other types of wetlands. Along with boardwalks and trails, each research reserve has plenty to offer the traveler.

These National Estuary Research Reserves (NERR) are one of the best kept secrets in the United States. The thirty reserves offer walking trails, boating trails, tours, and boardwalks that immerse visitors in the silent beauty of the estuary world. Many sightseers often miss these sites since they're rarely listed on tourist brochures. After all, these are scientific research and conservation areas. Entrances to the thousand-plus-acres of wetlands aren't grandiose either, but once inside, the beauty is overwhelming. From Bay St. Louis to Apalachicola, this different kind of beauty co-exists in contrast to glistening sands and sparkling waters.

MISSISSIPPI - GRAND BAY NATIONAL ESTUARINE RESEARCH RESERVE
MOSS POINT (NEAR ALABAMA STATE LINE)

Area Protected: 18,049 acres

Enter address **6005 Bayou Heron Rd. on GPS** to find entry off Hwy. 90

Shares area with Grand Bay National Wildlife Refuge

Bayous, marshes, pine savanna, freshwater marsh, pine
  forests; Oak Grove Birding Trail, Savanna Trail Boardwalk

Kayak, canoeing trails

Interpretative Center exhibit: Tobi, the diamond-backed
  terrapin swimming in his aquarium, and *Living on the
  Edge, Nature of Change;* audio oral histories with
  residents; Indoor and outdoor classrooms

Home to over 250 bird species; Sightings of bald eagles,
  swallow-tailed kites, bobcat, alligator, dolphin, osprey
  and manatee

READ: *Judas Burning* by Carolyn Haines

ALABAMA - WEEKS BAY NATIONAL ESTUARINE RESEARCH
RESERVE FAIRHOPE (SOUTH OF MOBILE)

Area Protected: 9,317 acres

Saltwater marshes, bottomlands, pitcher plant bog, bay, rivers

Boardwalks with viewing decks and interpretative signs

Nature Trail, Upland Trail, Ground Trail

Guided kayak expeditions

Education Center, Visitor Center

Science Center with pull-out drawer displays of skeletons

Exhibits and live wild animals

Home to brown pelican, eastern indigo snake, and
  Alabama red-bellied turtle

Recovering from Hurricane Sally damage in 2020

READ: *V for Victor* by Mark Childress

FLORIDA - APALACHICOLA NATIONAL ESTUARINE RESEARCH RESERVE
EASTPOINT (SOUTH OF APALACHICOLA)

Area Protected: 246,766 acres

River, bay, coastal hammock, freshwater marsh

Raised boardwalks marking distance to other rivers

100 miles of canoe and kayak trails

Home to 109 plant and 54 animal species listed as
  endangered, threatened, or of special concern including American alligator, Florida manatee, bald eagle,
  and loggerhead sea turtle.

5,400-square-foot nature center wIth three 1,000-gallon
  tanks; hands-on discovery room, gift shop

READ: *Out for Blood* by Michael Lister

Fairhope and its residents value the printed word so much they've honored books and education with sculptures. "A Matter of Fiction," a 5000-pound steel sculpture of an open book, was created by Birmingham artist Deedee Morrison and installed in 2012. It stands at the entrance of the Fairhope Public Library at 501 Fairhope Avenue.

FAIRHOPE, ALABAMA

This picturesque city that began as a utopian-socialist experiment in 1894 with a "fair hope" of success attracted writers from early on and continues to do so today. Some say Fairhope is home to more published authors per capita than any other city in the U.S. In his anthology *Stories from the Blue Moon Café*, author and resident Sonny Brewer points out once three local writers were on the *New York Times* Bestseller List simultaneously.

Fairhope reveres the written word. A massive steel sculpture of an open book graces the lawn of the Fairhope City Library. The 5000-pound piece created by Deedee Wallace, a Birmingham sculptor, is named "A Matter of Fiction." Another city art installation, a bronze sculpture commorating progressive teacher Marietta Johnson, sits at atop a bluff overlooking the Fairhope Municipal Pier. Johnson opened a progressive school in Fairhope in 1907.

In a joint venture of private and public funding, Fairhope honors writers with a center for writing arts and encourages them to stay awhile with a writer-in-residence program. **The Fairhope Center for the Writing Arts**, also called **Wolff Cottage**, a 1920's brick bungalow bordered with azaleas, is located at **9 North School Street,** behind the library. Upon acceptance, writers may stay as long as three months in the cozy cottage and hope for a Pulitzer Prize, like its first resident Rick Bragg. But Bragg wasn't the first Pulitzer Prize winner to claim Fairhope as home.

Already famous for his novel *The Jungle*, Upton Sinclair (1878-1968), moved his family to Fairhope in the winter of 1909-1910. He rented a bayside cottage with a long pier extending into Mobile Bay and made swimming part of his daily health regime. He wrote *Love's Pilgrimage*, an autobiographical novel published in 1911, in a tent on the bluff. C. W. Huntington's 1924 book *Enclaves of Economic Rent* includes an essay on land speculation in which Sinclair describes Fairhope's single-tax land rental system. In 1947, Sinclair won a Pulitzer Prize in fiction for *Dragon's Teeth*.

Sherwood Anderson (1876-1941) traveled south to "winter" in Alabama in February of 1920, the year after the publication of his critically acclaimed *Winesburg, Ohio*. After a short stay in Mobile, he moved to Fairhope, where he experienced a prolific period of writing fiction and poetry. He finished the first draft of the novel *Poor White* and began another book, *Many Marriages*. His wife, an artist, joined him, and they enjoyed river and bay cruises on excursion steamers. Sherwood Anderson also started painting with watercolor in Fairhope. In *Paris Notebook*, written in 1921, he described his Fairhope lodging as a "cabin on a strip of beach and beyond the beach the mouth of the river came down into the bay." That sounds like an idyllic estuary setting. (See Mobile, AL)

Fairhope resident Sonny Brewer, (1949-) journalist, novelist, former bookstore owner, and founder of the Fairhope Center for the Writing Arts, preserved some of Fairhope's utopian history in his debut novel *The Poet of Tolstoy Park* (2005). The book recounts the life of the eccentric Henry Stuart who moved to Fairhope from Idaho when doctors gave him only a year to live. Despite his tuberculosis diagnosis, the sixty-seven-year-old built a hurricane-proof, domed concrete hut and lived there eighteen years before leaving. When Ballantine Books Publishing opted to purchase his novel about Stuart, Brewer leased the concrete shelter and restored it. He revised the manuscript working on his laptop sitting at a small oak table inside the hut. Listed on the National Register of Historic Places, the hut is officially in Montrose, but blends into Fairhope at **22787 U.S. 98.** The site is easy to miss

When writer Sonny Brewer worked on his book *The Poet of Tolstoy Park* (2005), he revised the manuscript in the "hut" that inspired the novel. It is located in the parking lot of a business complex. Tolstoy Park was originally built and occupied by Henry Stuart in the 1920s. It is open to the public and located in Montrose, on the edge of Fairhope, at Highway 98 and Parker Road.

because it's hidden in plain sight, sitting **partially submerged in a parking lot under a giant oak.** Brewer has authored several other novels and collections plus *Stories from the Blue Moon Café*, an anthology filled with works by Fairhope writers.

New York Times bestselling writer Fannie Flagg (1944-), author of *Fried Green Tomatoes* and an Alabama native, wrote three books, including her first one, and the Oscar-nominated screenplay for *Fried Green Tomatoes* in Fairhope. She had lived nearby as a child when her family moved to Gulf Shores. When the actress-comedienne was living in New York and needed a place to getaway and write, she remembered Fairhope. The area often appears in her work and sometimes local residents appear, like the character selling tomatoes from a truck in *The All-Girl Filling Station's Last Reunion*. Other works are set in nearby Point Clear and Magnolia Springs. Flagg kept a home in Fairhope for many years, still visits, and has done readings at the **Page & Palette, 32 S. Section St.** She describes Fairhope as "a magical place" in a *New York Times* interview. (See Gulf Shores, Point Clear, and Magnolia Springs, AL)

Rick Bragg (1959-), Pulitzer Prize winning feature writer and Alabama native, has written ten books, including two *New York Times* bestsellers. Magazine readers know him as a featured columnist in *Southern Living* and

Wolff Cottage, operated by Fairhope Center for the Writing Arts, is located behind the Fairhope Public Library at 9 North School Street. The one bedroom, one bath cottage provides a home for visiting writers-in-residence in a program established in 2004. The program, which began with quarterly opportunities, now welcomes a different writer each month. Writers-in-residence are asked to provide one community program during their stay. The cottage was built in the 1920s.

Garden & Gun. Bragg was Wolff Cottage's first writer-in-residence and keeps a second home in Fairhope. **Sunset Pointe at Fry Creek Marina, 831 N. Section St.,** features a Rick Bragg "Ode to Grouper" fish sandwich on its menu. The fish sandwich's name is a nod to his *Garden & Gun* feature, a finalist for the James Beard Award for Personal Essay. Bragg often writes personal essays about Fairhope for internationally read publications as the *Smithsonian* and the *New York Times.*

New York Times and *USA Today* bestselling author Julie Cantrell, a Louisiana native with Mississippi ties, calls Fairhope home. She is the author of *Into the Free, The Feathered Bone, When Mountains Move* and *Perennials,* all award winning novels. She's also an editor, ghostwriter, TedX speaker, creative writing instructor, and managing director of national writers' group, Story Summit.

Fairhope's Ronald Everett Capps' novel *Off Magazine Street* (2004) was adapted for the film *A Love Song for Bobby Long* starring John Travolta and Scarlett Johansson. The book is set in New Orleans.

In the book *Man and Mission: E.B. Gaston and the Origins of the Fairhope Single Tax Colony,* the visionary who founded the colony of Fairhope in 1894 is profiled by his grandson Paul M. Gaston (1928-2019), a civil rights activist, Southern historian, and college professor. The younger Gaston, born in

Two storybook castles located on the same property at **457 Oak Avenue, Fairhope,** are a private residence and an Air BnB owned by the family of Craig Turner Sheldon (1917-1997), celebrated builder, veteran, artist, sculptor, writer, columnist, and satirist. For nearly 40 years Sheldon wrote the semi-weekly column "Knee Deep in Fly Creek with Sheldon" for the *Fairhope Courier*. Both the local history museum and library have exhibits of his work. The homes are the ultimate fairytale castles complete with miniature drawbridges, a tower, ponds, fairy gardens, dragons, and whimsical roof lines. Sheldon used his imagination to repurpose materials to create Sheldon Castle, while son-in-law Dean Mosher, created the neighboring Mosher Castle. Boom Castle, the third whimsical structure, built in 2020, is also a private residence.

Fairhope, also wrote *Women of Fair Hope,* along with numerous other social and academic works.

Readers in England and Australia are big fans of mystery writer Jack Kerley (1951-), who uses coastal Alabama for the setting of many of his novels. Kerley often spends three months at a time in Fairhope living in a home belonging to his parents. He uses the eccentricities, exaggerations, and hot, humid weather of the South to create psychological thrillers. He's written over a dozen novels, printed in at least ten different languages.

Lawyer Frank Turner Hollon (1963-) found literary success first in Fairhope but was soon picked up by a California publisher. He's written ten novels while maintaining his law practice in nearby Robertsdale and serving as a prosecutor for Gulf Shores. His novel *Blood and Circumstance* was made into a film by the same name, while his first novel *Life is a Strange Place* was adapted into the movie *Barry Munday*.

With so many noteworthy writers living in Fairhope, the city piqued the interest of the great-grandson of Joseph Pulitzer. Mac Pulitzer's dream was to build a boutique hotel next to a Pulitzer Library housing copies of the Pulitzer Prize winners and finalists — novels, short stories, plays, poetry. In 2011 he announced Fairhope as the location for his dream. The press release described Fairhope as "Home to two Pulitzer Prize-winning authors, two Pulitzer Prize nominees, fourteen Oscar nominations, six Academy Awards, four *New York Times* bestselling authors and many other acclaimed authors." Sadly, Pulitzer's utopian dream lost its funding. Hopefully, there's a Fairhope writer planning to tell the story of Mac Pulitzer's shattered dream.

A sculpture of Marietta Johnson, a progressive education reformer and founder of Fairhope's Organic School for Education, is located in Utopia Park on a bluff overlooking Mobile Bay. The three-piece ensemble includes a seated Johnson reading to two young children. The "Marietta Johnson Memorial" was created by sculptors Fran Neumann, Barbara Casey, and Richard Arnold and dedicated in 1997.

The March 2019 memorial service following the death of bestselling author W.E.B. Griffin (William Butterworth III) was held at picturesque Saint Francis at the Point Anglican Church at 17280 Scenic Hwy. 98 in Point Clear.

POINT CLEAR, ALABAMA

Addresses distinguishing Point Clear and Fairhope are nebulous. In Point Clear, front yards face Mobile Bay and backyards face the highway. To have a Point Clear address (at the backyard entrance), residents must also have a post office box, otherwise, the address will read Fairhope.

One distinguished Point Clear resident was author William Edmund Butterworth III (1929-2019), who wrote or co-authored more than 250 books, many as W.E.B. Griffin, his most-used pseudonym. Though many readers know him for the novelization of the *M.A.S.H.* books, others know him for his military, political, detective, spy, counterterrorism, or young adult books. For business and branding reasons, he used twelve different pen names due to the vast number of novels he could produce in a year.

He was both a *New York Times* and *The Wall Street Journal* number one bestselling author. He was born in New Jersey, but after being stationed at Fort Rucker, Alabama, settled in the Fairhope-Point Clear area. Later, he split his time between Alabama and Buenos Aires. More than 50 million copies of his books are in print in more than ten different languages. Before his death, he lived at **17697 Scenic Highway 98, Point Clear,** about four houses up the road from **The Grand Hotel.** He enjoyed golfing at **The Grand's Lakewood Golf Course.** Butterworth's memorial service was held at the picturesque **Saint Francis at the Point Anglican Church in Point Clear.** His son, William Edmund Butterworth IV, is continuing his father's writing legacy, just not in Fairhope.

Most famous for creating *Forrest Gump*, Winston Groom (1943-2020), lived most of his life in Point Clear. Groom wrote fourteen books, both fiction and nonfiction, three of which were made into

Point Clear residents enjoy walking the scenic pathway at The Grand Hotel which overlooks Mobile Bay. From here, the historic Middle Bay Lighthouse is visible. The lighthouse is depicted on the cover of Jennifer Paddock's novel *Point Clear.*

films. Groom, by the way, did not coin the phrase "life is like a box of chocolates." The line was added by a Hollywood screen writer.

Sookie, the Southern protagonist in Fannie Flagg's novel *The All-Girl Filling Station's Last Reunion,* claims Point Clear as her hometown. Though Sookie's home address, 526 Bay Street, is fictional, **The Colony** restaurant, where Sookie and her mother enjoy crab cakes, is located at **104 N. Section St., Fairhope.** The characters in the book dine out often. Some restaurant locations are authentic, like the **Fairhope Inn at 63 S. Church, Fairhope.** Sandra's Sidewalk Café could be **Sandra's Place at 218 Fairhope. Ave., Fairhope,** a four-minute walk from **Page & Palette Bookstore, 32 S. Section St.,** also mentioned in the book. The **Waffle House** where Sookie regularly meets her psychiatrist, is located at **373 S. Greeno Rd., Fairhope;** their alternative meeting spot, **Ruby Tuesday, 901 Fairhope Ave., Fairhope,** is permanently closed. Several restaurant names, however, are clever creations by the author. The book often mentions The Grand Hotel and its amenities, especially

The Grand Hotel in Point Clear has an onsite historian who oversees the history displays and leads tours. One display case includes a shelf of novels set at The Grand.

dining and large-scale events. Sookie's mother even preplans her own funeral and memorial reception for the **Grand Ballroom at the Grand Hotel, One Grand Blvd., Point Clear.** (See Magnolia Springs and Fairhope, AL)

Poet Sidney Lanier (1842-1881) spent the winter of 1865 at Point Clear on Mobile Bay at the home of his uncle while recuperating from tuberculosis. Some accounts say the pine scent and bay breezes restored Lanier, who had contracted TB when held prisoner during the Civil War. (See Mobile, AL)

When novelist William Campbell (1893-1954), who wrote under the pen name William March, was found suffering from depression in New York in 1947, his friends from Mobile packed him up and brought him to a suite at the Grand Hotel in Point Clear to recover. Unfortunately, the hotel's guest records are missing from that year, but allegedly Campbell lived at the hotel for eleven months until healthy enough to relocate to Mobile.

Novelist Mark Childress (1957-) includes a hotel much like The Grand in his World War II novel *V for Victor*, in which a Nazi U-boat is spotted in Mobile Bay. Still today, some locals claim that a Nazi sub *did* appear in Mobile Bay. Though that may be myth, it's a fact that in the final push to end the war, the hotel itself, played an important role. Operation Ivory Soap maneuvers trained offshore at Point Clear in a classified military operation; the hotel was the training base. The Army Air Corps operation was managed from

Suite 1108 of The Grand Hotel. The resort's Thompson Suite is named after Lt. Col. Matthew Thompson, who ran the floating aircraft repair-ship operation, appropriately named after a soap that "floats." The 170-year-old hotel, affectionately called the "Queen of Southern Resorts," is part of Marriott International's Autograph Collection of Hotels and their **Grand Hotel Golf Resort & Spa is located at One Grand Blvd.** They have an onsite historian who gives tours and has a display of books in which the hotel plays a part.

Author Jennifer Paddock, who taught tennis at The Grand for thirteen years, set her novel *Point Clear* at The Grand Hotel. In the book, the main character rides out Hurricane Ivan alone in the hotel. The book's cover features a photograph of the historic Middle Bay Lighthouse visible from The Grand Hotel. Paddock has written two other novels and been published in the *New York Times* and *Tennis View Magazine*.

The Grand Hotel is also the setting for *New York Times* bestselling author Andy Andrews' latest book, *The Noticer Returns*. Andrews (1959-), an inspirational speaker, is also the author of *The Heart Mender*, a fascinating account of WWII German subs in Mobile Bay; he lives in nearby Orange Beach where he discovered the submariner's artifacts that inspired the book.

Anne George (1927-2001), former Alabama Poet Laureate and author of the *Southern Sisters Mystery Series*, set one of her novels, *This One and Magic Life*, in Point Clear at The Grand Hotel. (See Destin, FL)

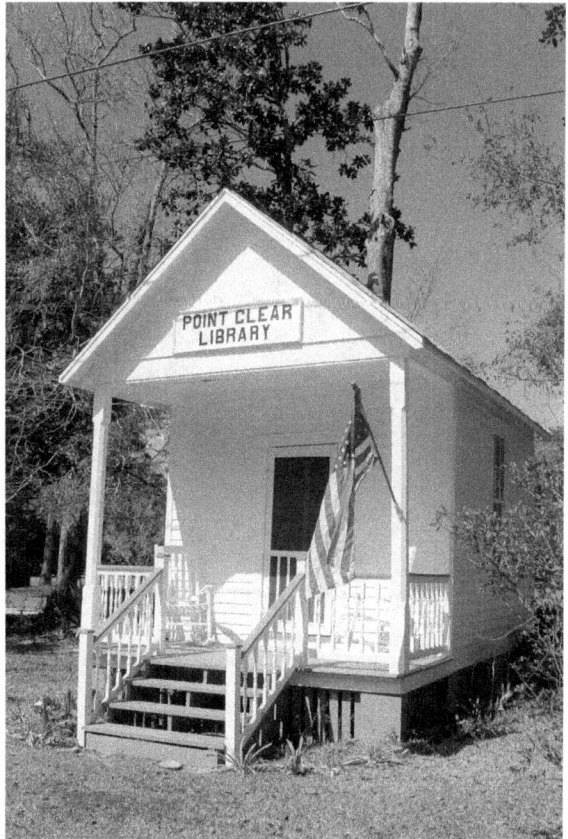

Once authenticated by *Ripley's Believe It or Not!* as the World's Smallest Library, this structure was saved from demolition by the father of author Watt Key. It's located in the "backyard" of the Key residence but visible from Highway 98 in Point Clear. Front yards face Mobile Bay.

Just a short drive from The Grand is what was once named the World's Smallest Library. In 1920, *Ripley's Believe It or Not!* verified that the 13×14-foot structure with over 2000 books was, indeed, the world's smallest library. The quaint one room building has a front porch and front screen door. The library, which was relocated to **16903 Scenic Highway 98**, sits behind the home of the parents of popular author Watt Key (1970-). Watt's father is responsible for saving the little library and restoring it.

Watt Key's 2010 debut novel *Alabama Moon* was turned into a movie starring John Goodman and is popular with both Alabama teachers and young adult readers. (Grown-ups like it too). *Alabama Moon* won the 2007 E.B. White Award and the 2006 Parent's Choice Award along with garnering fourteen other library and literary honors. Key has written nearly a dozen young adult novels, many like *Bay Boys*, inspired by his childhood growing up along Mobile Bay at Point Clear.

Author Fannie Flagg's *A Redbird Christmas* is set in a quiet town patterned after Magnolia Springs. The shady Magnolia Springs Bed & Breakfast, with rocking chairs on the front porch, is Tripadvisor's number one-ranked B & B in Alabama. Authentically Southern in architecture, the home was built in 1897.

MAGNOLIA SPRINGS, ALABAMA

"Lost River" the fictional setting in Fannie Flagg's popular novel *A Redbird Christmas* is patterned after Magnolia Springs, the only place in America where mail is still delivered by boat. Tree-lined streets, lush lawns, and historic cottages and homes portray a community lost in time. Many of the sprawling homes back up to the meandering Magnolia River. For a closer view of the river, take a stroll down **Magnolia Landing's boardwalk off Magnolia Highway behind Jesse's Restaurant (14770 Oak St.).** It's a short walk down the elevated walkway, above a swampy, wooded area, to the landing and viewing platform. If it's a hot summer day, you'll see locals cooling off as they float carefree along the river in innertubes.

Jesse's Restaurant (14770 Oak St.) which is in the old post office, also encompasses the former Moore Bros. Village Market built in 1922. Diners eat in the store portion of the restaurant or on the covered porch. The World War II novel *V for Victor* by Southern writer Mark Childress features a closing chapter set in the original village market. Childress lived in Magnolia Springs for three years in the late 1980s. Nearby Weeks Bay and the Magnolia River play a major part in the novel in which a sixteen-year-old boy discovers a Nazi submarine in the bay and a ring of German spies on land.

Weeks Bay National Estuarine Research Reserve, 11300 Hwy. 98,

Jesse's Restaurant, which includes portions of Magnolia Springs' old post office and village market, is mentioned in Mark Childress' 1998 book *V for Victor*. Childress lived in Magnolia Springs while writing the novel.

Magnolia Springs is the only town left in the United States where the mail is delivered by boat. The Magnolia River is featured in novels by Fannie Flagg and Mark Childress and is visible from the Magnolia River Bridge or by walking the boardwalk to Magnolia Landing behind Jesse's Restaurant.

between **Fairhope and Foley, just west of the Fish River Bridge**, brings the novel's watery settings — the Magnolia River, Weeks Bay, Mobile Bay, and the mouth of the Gulf — to life. The Weeks Bay Reserve offers several boardwalks with great observation decks for viewing the bay. It's especially picturesque near sunset. In spring, the pitcher plant bog on **County Road 17** not far from the Interpretive Center on **Highway 98** is in full bloom.

GULF SHORES, ALABAMA

Gulf Shores along the Gulf of Mexico must have been an exciting beat for a young reporter after hurricanes devastated the area in both 1979 and 1985, each time the city restoring its beauty. One such reporter, Brad Watson, tracked Hurricane Elena as he flew with the Air Force storm trackers. He later covered the storm's aftermath and wrote feature stories ranging from rattlesnake hunters to shark fishermen to dangers on the beach. Perhaps these stories fueled his imagination for his award-winning fiction. Watson (1955 -2020) spent part of the 1980s and 1990s reporting for several newspapers along the Alabama and Florida coasts. A Mississippi native, as a child he vacationed with his family along both the Alabama and Mississippi coasts. As an adult he lived in Gulf Shores.

Before continuing his education and becoming an award-winning novelist, Watson filled his life with varied experiences — husband and father while in high school, struggling actor, bar manager, and Hollywood garbage truck driver. No doubt the stories he covered on the beach added to his bank of human knowledge. Watson's first collection won the Sue Kaufman Prize for First Fiction; his first novel *The Heaven of Mercury* was named a finalist for the National Book Award, PEN/Faulkner Award, and recipient of both the Harper Lee Award and the Southern Book Critics Circle Award. Most of his short stories and novels are set along the Gulf Coast.

Watson went on to serve as writer-in-residence at several universities, teach writing at Harvard, and become the creative writing program director at the University of Wyoming. (See Pensacola, FL)

Fannie Flagg's family moved to Gulf Shores when she was a fifth grader. Coastal Alabama features in much of her work. (See Fairhope, Magnolia Springs, and Point Clear, AL)

One of author-songwriter Jimmy Buffett's favorite restaurants is in Gulf Shores. **LuLu's (200 E. 25th Ave.)** is owned by Buffett's sister Lucy, herself a noted cookbook author, chef, and restauranteur.

TOP 10 FESTIVALS

1. PETER ANDERSON (MS)

The largest arts and crafts festival in Mississippi has been around for more than 40 years. The first weekend in November people come in droves to the quaint artist town of Ocean Springs for this outdoor festival. Crowd sizes soar up to 150,000 people with more than 400 artists, crafters and food vendors setting up shop over the weekend. More than 150 participating shops, galleries, and businesses surround the local and visiting artists. The festival has a street fair vibe with exhibitors from around the country, and the visiting artists bring quality work since it's a competitive, juried show.

2. CRUISIN' THE COAST (MS)

Billed as the "World's Largest Block Party," this week-long October car show incorporates music and entertainment, car shows and swap meets, sock hops and street parties, car competitions, auctions, and parades with events in every town along the Mississippi Coast – from Bay St. Louis to Moss Point. In 2021 in a pandemic, more than 9400 antique and classic cars and hot rods showed up for the 25th anniversary of the festival which began as a nostalgic celebration of America's love for classic cars and music. Cruisin' the Coast has a trunk load of accolades including being twice honored as one of "100 Events for the Year" by the American Bus Association. Cruisin' the Coast was named a Southern Travel Treasure by AAA's magazine, and the Governor of Mississippi and Southeast Tourism Society have also honored the show. Twelve car clubs and over 700 volunteers make this lively event possible.

3. BLESSING OF THE FLEET (AL)

Thousands of visitors come to the small fishing village of Bayou La Batre the first weekend in May. Since 1949, fishermen have officially had their boats blessed in a fleet ceremony that has transformed into a two-day festival organized by St. Margaret's Parish. Visitors and residents enjoy music, a land parade and a boat parade, a gumbo cook-off, a decorated boat contest, coronation of a queen, and a variety of food booths. Refugee Vietnamese "boat people" and their descendants who made this area their home after the Vietnam war, operate a popular food booth featuring Vietnamese fare. One-fourth of the population of small Bayou La Batre is Asian. Decorated boats, mostly shrimp boats, receive a blessing from the Archbishop of the Diocese of Mobile as they glide by the dock. The festival is based on the Old World religious tradition of fishermen acknowledging God and asking for a bountiful harvest.

4. BILLY BOWLEGS PIRATE INVASION & DOWNTOWN PARTY (FL)

This multi-day summer event in Fort Walton Beach has been happening since 1950. It begins as Captain Billy Bowlegs and his elaborately costumed band of pirates arrive by pirate ship to take over the city. Hundreds of local boats fill the Sound as the pirates kidnap the mayor and city council in a reenactment that includes cannon fire, musketeers, music, and plenty of pirates. The festivities include a Saturday festival with family activities following the pirate landing, downtown party, torchlight parade, evening fireworks, and a pub crawl. The event is named after the legendary pirate who led raids against the Spanish territories in this part of Florida. His band included Native American warriors, frontiersmen, and former slaves.

5. BLUE ANGELS HOMECOMING (FL)

Every November this four-day free air show on Pensacola Beach celebrates the return of the world-famous U.S. Navy aerobatic flight demonstration team to its winter home at Pensacola's Naval Air Station. The beach event includes aerial performances leading up to a daily Blue Angels flyover and aerobatic feats of wonder. The air show weekend is surrounded by a calendar of cultural events which are part of Foo Foo Fest (that's a name for entertainment on a Navy carrier). Foo Foo opens with the nationally acclaimed Great Gulf Coast Arts Fest. The outdoor juried art show features an international artist as well as more than a hundred exhibiting artists from around the country.

6. FRANK BROWN INTERNATIONAL SONGWRITERS FESTIVAL (AL-FL)

For more than 35 years, aspiring and veteran songwriters and musicians get a chance to be heard and tell the stories behind their lyrics at the Frank Brown festival. Songwriters showcase their songs before live audiences at varying venues from Orange Beach to Gulf Shores to Pensacola. As many as 15,000 music lovers attend the 11-day, free festival to hear up to 200 songwriters perform, sometimes in tents, on the beach, in bars, at small clubs, and at the famous Flora-Bama Lounge, which sits on the state line between Florida and Alabama. The songwriters' stories inspired the 2020 documentary *Stories in Rhyme: The Songwriters of the Flora-Bama Lounge.* It's the longest-running songwriters' festival in the country.

7. FLORIDA SEAFOOD FESTIVAL (FL)

This Apalachicola fest takes the best of every other local festival and wraps it up into one big shindig centered around the town's seafood industry. Along with plenty of seafood prepared by local cooks, there's a blessing of the fleet, parade, royalty, arts and crafts fair, 5K run, carnival rides, maritime exhibits, and live musical entertainment. The two-day event is Florida's oldest maritime event. Tens of thousands attend the event held at the oak-shaded Battery Park on the waterfront of this historic town. Contests include the distinctive and different Oyster Eating and Oyster Shucking events and the Blue Crab Races. They've been crowning Miss Florida Seafood since 1964, but the festival traces its origin to 1914. It ranks as one of the top 15 small town festivals in America, and the number six oyster festival in the world. The best part may be the locally caught seafood prepared and served at the local food booths operated by nonprofit organizations.

The Flora-Bama Lounge Package Store and Oyster Bar, located on Highway 98 at the Florida-Alabama state line, draws gigantic crowds for both a songwriter's festival and the mullet toss.

8. FLORA-BAMA MULLET TOSS (AL-FL)

This giant beach party features a unique competition — throw a dead mullet (fish) across the state line from Alabama into Florida. Hosted by the legendary Flora-Bama Lounge, Package & Oyster Bar, the Mullet Toss attracts as many as 35,000 visitors from across the country to Perdido Key. Competitors, organized into divisions including one for kids, throw a mullet as far as 189 feet on one of the most gorgeous beaches in the world. Just like the first mullet toss in 1986, the winner still gets a free mullet dinner at a local restaurant. There's also a bikini contest, plenty of beverages from the Flora-Bama, and live music that goes on into the wee hours. There's a fee to participate and park, but the event raises about $20,000 annually for local charities. Afterwards, the dead mullet are fed to birds.

9. THUNDER BEACH MOTORCYCLE RALLY (FL)

The thundering sound of thousands of motorcycles rumbles into Panama City Beach for the "Most Biker Friendly Free Rally in the United States." Over 60,000 people attend the twice-a-year, multi-day festival held at venues around the city and the beach. Bikers shop in tents filled with motorcycle themed merchandise, enter their bikes in shows, ride in a memorial parade and participate in special events like a Poker Run. In the Poker Run, participants ride to designated locations (shops, pubs, bars, restaurants) where they draw cards hoping for a good enough poker hand to win the event. Other activities include a beauty pageant, live music, and an arts and crafts show.

10. NATIONAL SHRIMP FESTIVAL (AL)

Gulf Shores welcomes more than 250,000 people to eat shrimp, shop a massive art fair with hundreds of exhibiting artists, and listen to live music for the Shrimp Festival. The October weekend event is free, and features plenty of family activities, though it's hard to maneuver the stroller through the crowds on the soft sand. But it's the sand that makes the Sand Sculpture contest a highlight. And, of course, there's a Miss Shrimp Festival pageant. Almost 50 years old, this festival is one of the top five tourist attractions in Alabama, a bronze winner for Best Overall Festival from Southeast Festivals and Events, and on *Southern Living* magazine's best festival list.

Florida Panhandle

Florida

Ernest Hemingway, Jack Kerouac, Zora Neale Hurston, Harriet Beecher Stowe, Elmore Leonard, John D. MacDonald, and Marjorie Kinnan Rawlings all wrote and earned fame while living in Florida – albeit none in the same place. They were scattered across Florida's 65,577 square miles. In true Florida festival style, all these places celebrate the literature of the Sunshine State.

The Miami Book Fair, the largest literary festival in the U.S., lasts eight days and welcomes 300-plus authors from around the world to hawk their books.

The Florida Heritage and Book Festival in historic St. Augustine names the Florida Writer of the Year and is one of Florida's Best Twelve Annual Events right along with the Mullet Toss and the Frog Leg Festival. St. Petersburg remembers the oldies with its annual antiquarian book fair.

For more than thirty years, the small town of Eatonville has honored Zora Neale Hurston with Zora!, a festival celebrating African American contributions to arts and humanities.

And, only in Florida, can men compete in an Ernest Hemingway lookalike contest in a Key West bar.

On a more serious note, the Florida Book Awards annually honor the best books written by Floridians in eleven categories, including cookbooks and children's literature. The Florida Humanities Council bestows an annual Lifetime Literary Achievement Award. In Orlando, aspiring authors can be writers-in-residence and live in Jack Kerouac's house.

Floridians are encouraged to nominate poets for the state poet laureate position, originally a lifetime appointment. Therefore, the state has honored only four poets laureate. The newest job description requires a minimum of four years as poet laureate.

Contemporary authors cluster around Tampa, Orlando, and Miami, but the Panhandle adds plenty of flavor to the diverse mix of Florida voices. In Pensacola readers can experience the hometown of the author who made "Weird Florida" famous while he also documented environmentalists' efforts to save the state's manatees and panthers. And down the road near Apalachicola, literary travelers can view the prison that inspired a novelist to write twenty-five plus novels about a prison chaplain solving murders. Only in the Sunshine State.

THE FLORIDA PANHANDLE

Northwest Florida boasts 150 miles of sandy beaches, some pristine and untouched by commercial development. Continually redefined by visitor bureaus and tourism agencies, most counties of the Florida Panhandle are different from typical-tourist Florida. The gorgeous white, sugar-sand beaches and crystal clear, see-through green waters are now called The Emerald Coast, a much classier moniker than its earliest name — the Redneck Riviera. During the area's evolution, a section called The Miracle Strip boasted roadside goofy golf courses, amusement parks, and snake and alligator farms, while a few condominiums down Highway 98 in Destin, the luckiest fishing village in the world began redecorating itself to look like the French Riviera.

The Emerald Coast includes the beaches near Pensacola, Navarre, Fort Walton Beach, Destin, and Panama City along Highway 98. Skirting off Highway 98 between Destin and Panama City is Scenic Highway 30A, home to villages including Blue Mountain Beach, Grayton Beach, WaterColor, Seaside, Seagrove Beach, WaterSound, Alys Beach, Seacrest, and Rosemary Beach.

After Scenic Highway 30A rejoins Highway 98, The Forgotten Coast begins. This pristine area of the wild Florida coastline includes remote beaches, towns like Port St. Joe, Apalachicola, and Indian Pass. Whether it's The Forgotten Coast, The Miracle Strip, or The Emerald Coast, Florida's Panhandle offers unique vacation spots, places to escape and write, and endless opportunities for memorable settings.

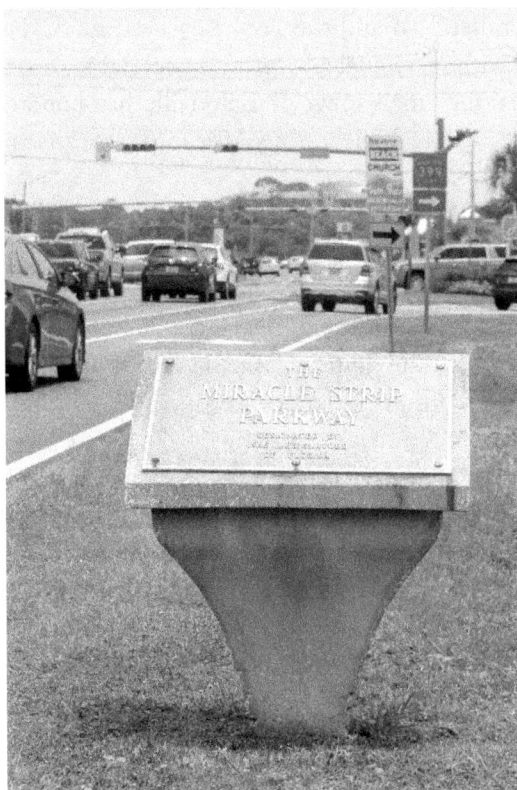

The brand of Florida's Panhandle is everchanging. This 1965 Florida Legislature marker designated Highway 98 in Navarre as "The Miracle Strip."

HURRICANE WIPEOUTS

On Aug. 15, 1559, Spanish explorer and Conquistador Tristan de Luna landed near present day Pensacola, establishing the first European settlement in America. On Sept. 19, a hurricane destroyed the settlement along with de Luna's fleet. Survivors tried to reestablish the settlement but abandoned it in 1561. Therefore, St. Augustine, founded in 1565, claims the title "America's Oldest City." Pensacola is "America's Oldest Settlement."

Northwest Florida remains the most hurricane-prone area in Florida, according to Universal Property & Casualty Insurance. *Statistically, the Florida Panhandle alone has had more hurricanes than any state in the union.*

PENSACOLA AND PENSACOLA BEACH, FLORIDA

Lauded as the #4 Book Lovers' Town in the U.S. by Explore. com in 2024, Pensacola is America's oldest settlement. The city has inspired an abundance of fictional, historical and archaeological works. Adding to the lore, naval aviators, veterans, and war heroes have penned volumes about Pensacola as The Cradle of Navy Aviation. The city is home to scores of noteworthy songwriters and musicians and boasts a lively literary scene with at least four organizations focused on writing. Emerald Coast Writers (originally West Florida Literary Federation, Inc.), a nonprofit organization with a mission to preserve the literary history of Northwest Florida, collects, catalogs, and shelves books by regional writers in the Dr. Francis Patrick Cassidy Writer's Resource Library in the **Cultural Center at 400 S. Jefferson.** The nonprofit also hosts the lively Books By the Bay book festival every March.

Historic Pensacola reveres and recognizes good storytellers. **The Appleyard Storytelling Cottage at 213 East Zaragoza** in Historic Pensacola Village features storytellers describing local history, originally with its namesake himself spinning the tales. The cottage is named after local historian John Appleyard (1922-2020) who published over 100 books, including accounts of the area's history and citizens, along with 1900-era Pensacola police stories. **The Rose Garden Storytelling Circle behind Pensacola Museum of History (330 Jefferson, at the intersection of Jefferson and Government across from the Pensacola Cultural Center)** also has costumed actors reciting stories of historic Pensacolians.

Writers and readers hoping to get chummy with an editor can pose for a photo with J. Earle Bowden's likeness around the corner from Bodacious Books. Bowden, local editor, cartoonist, and author is heralded as The Father of the Gulf Islands National Seashore.

Standing at the **Rose Garden Storytelling Circle**, visitors can see the **J. Earle Bowden Building at 120 Church Street.** The restored Art-Deco style building, operated by the University of West Florida Historic Trust, is named after newspaperman and political cartoonist Jesse Earle Bowden (1928-2015), a devout supporter of the preservation of historic buildings as well as the Gulf Islands National Seashore. A bronze statue of Bowden is a few blocks away, located at the corner of **Jefferson and Intendencia Streets in J. Earle Bowden Plaza** within Southtowne, a shopping and apartment complex where the offices of the *Pensacola News Journal* once stood. While editor of the newspaper, Bowden walked the newspaper beat daily along Jefferson Street. Aficionados of newspapers and printing presses will appreciate the reconstructed 1900's pressroom highlighting Pensacola's newspaper history in **The Museum of Commerce at 201 East Zaragoza** in Historic Pensacola Village.

America's first naturalist and environmentalist author-artist, William Bartram (1739-1823) is commemorated with a trail that passes through eight states. A portion of the William Bartram Trail winds through the Pensacola area, which Bartram briefly visited in 1775 while studying inland waterways. The most popular and scenic spot honoring him is **William Bartram Park (211 Bayfront Parkway),** a 2.6-acre public park near downtown's historic district. It has sidewalks and a picnic area overlooking Pensacola Bay plus a nice view of a marina and the bay. Bartram described Pensacola Bay in his 1791 book *Travels* as "safe and large enough to care for the combined havens of the world." The park sits across the street from historic Seville Square and next to the headquarters of the Florida Archaeology Network. (See Mobile, AL)

Four other historical markers plot Bartram's travels in the area. The signs,

William Bartram Memorial Park, located across Bayfront Parkway from Historic Seville Square in Pensacola, honors the brief presence of botanist William Bartram in Pensacola in 1775. The West Florida territorial governor invited Bartram to stay for dinner at his home across from what is now a yacht harbor. Bartram declined, made observations about Pensacola Bay, and headed back to Alabama.

erected by local garden clubs, are located at the entrance to the **Oar House Restaurant, 1000 South Pace Blvd; Fort Pickens picnic area on Pensacola Beach; Highway 98 beside Perdido Bay at Lillian Bridge (south FL side); and the Alabama Welcome Station on I-10 westbound** from Pensacola.

There's a chance poet Sidney Lanier (1842-1881) visited the Pensacola area when writing the touring guide, *Florida: Its Scenery, Climate and History*. In the chapter "Ocklawaha River" he compares the steamboat *Marion*, on which he is traveling, to a Pensacola gopher turtle. In the guidebook, Lanier predicts Pensacola will become an important place as he delineates the railway connections that pass through, including the Perdido Railway, a nine-mile stretch of rail connecting Pensacola Bay with Perdido Bay. He describes Pensacola as ten miles inland, quite different from today, and mentions Santa Rosa Island and the community of Warrington. There's no evidence this poet tour-guide ever visited Pensacola, however, he praised "the beauty of the gulf coastal bays" and "fine fish and oysters." Of course, Lanier could have visited after the Civil War, since he lived nearby in Alabama for a while. (See Point Clear, AL)

Pulitzer Prize winning poet Wallace Stevens (1879-1955) visited

Pensacola in 1919. A noted modernistic poet, Stevens never quit his day job, rising to Vice President of Hartford Accident and Indemnity Insurance Company in Hartford, Conn. Though his first poetry was published in 1915 and his first book in 1923, the bulk of his poetry was written after age fifty. His business brought him to Florida for more than twenty years. He described his anticipation to see Pensacola in a letter to his wife written on January 17, 1919, while riding the train from Jacksonville to Houston — "Summer never completely fades out in Northern Florida, but, of course, it is very different from Southern Florida which is four hundred miles away. Tomorrow morning I change cars, I believe, in Pensacola and have several hours to spare."

Lovers of historical fiction will enjoy walking the streets of Historic Pensacola and viewing the sites mentioned in Marilyn Turk's novel *Rekindled Light*. The novel is set in Pensacola in 1869. Turk's characters attend worship services at **Old Christ Church,** built in 1832 and located at **405 S. Adams St.** The main character's home is patterned after **The Barkley House,** circa 1835, located at **410 South Florida Blanca,** within walking distance of **Old Christ Church.** Characters visit **Seville Square at 311 Government St.,** facing the bay. Within walking distance of their home is **Garden Street** where townspeople once planted their gardens. As characters attempt to recover the stolen Pensacola Lighthouse lens, action takes place at **Fort Barrancas,** built in 1839, and **Fort Pickens,** built in 1834. Both forts are open to the public, but little remains of **Fort McRee,** the third fort mentioned in the novel. The **Pensacola Lighthouse,** complete with 177 steps as described in the book, is located at **2081 Radford Blvd.** on the grounds of **Naval Air Station-Pensacola.** It is open for tours. Characters also picnic on **Santa Rosa Island,** where picnics are still possible, thanks to the **Gulf Islands National Seashore.** (See Niceville, FL)

Before Duchess of Windsor Wallis Warfield Simpson (1896-1986) married the man who abdicated the throne of England for her, she lived in Pensacola. In 1916 she moved to Pensacola to live with her cousin, who was married to a U.S. Navy captain and new head of the Pensacola Air Base. Wallis met her first husband Win Spencer, a U.S. Navy aviator stationed in Pensacola. At one point the couple lived in a stately Victorian Queen Anne house at **52 Gonzales St.** It remains a private residence. Numerous fictional accounts and biographies of her life have been written, many including references to her time in Pensacola as the wife of a navy pilot. *The Heart Has Its Reasons: The Memoirs of the Duchess of Windsor* (1956), an autobiography, includes her account of time in Pensacola, her marriage, and life in the navy yard.

In Danger's Path, Book Eight in the Corps series by W.E.B. Griffin

The William Johnson house at 52 West Gonzalez in Pensacola was the residence of Wallis Warfield Simpson (then Spencer) when she was married to Naval aviator Win Spencer. The original clawfoot tub on the first floor is where her drunken husband tied her up on three occasions.

(1929-2019), includes scenes set at **Naval Air Station-Pensacola**. (See Fairhope, AL)

Brad Watson (1955-2020) worked for several newspapers along the Florida and Alabama coasts and flew with the Blue Angels on one reporting assignment. Later he was a writer-in-residence and taught at the **University of West Florida, 11100 University Parkway**. His first collection, *Last Days of the Dog-Men*, won the Sue Kaufman Award for first fiction. His first novel, *The Heaven of Mercury*, was a finalist for the National Book Award. (See Gulf Shores, AL)

Several contemporary women authors claim Pensacola as their hometown or have made it home. Joshilyn Jackson (1968-) was born in nearby Fort Walton Beach into a military family. After age nine, she grew up in Pensacola and graduated from **Booker T. Washington High School, 6000 College Parkway.** A bestselling author of women's fiction, Southern fiction, and psychological suspense, Jackson has written ten novels and her work is translated into a dozen languages. Her 2019 novel *Never Have I Ever* takes place in Pensacola. Though the Pensacola neighborhood and eateries are fictitious, the majesty and the eeriness of the deep-sea diving wrecks is realistic. Jackson personifies the ocean as having moods. When the main character takes a group of tourists diving at the wreck of an English freighter, the description of the water's buoyancy, a green moray eel, a little sea turtle soaring over the eel, a silvery cloud of small baitfish, and blue-and-white damselfish is breathtaking. The Pensacola setting works perfectly since the area is the site of six shipwrecks, one on the Florida Underwater Archeology Preserve. The underwater site of an "English freighter" may have been inspired by a popular dive site off the Pensacola coast which locals call the "Russian freighter." Named the *San Pablo*, the 315-foot-long shipwreck sits in about eighty feet of water and is part of the Florida Panhandle Shipwreck Trail. Fishermen love the site because of its array of fish, while divers enjoy the artifacts and the wreck itself, which was sunk by the U.S. government in 1944 near Costa Rica and refloated off the coast of Pensacola. In *Never Have I Ever*, Jackson also adds a nod to the popular Pensacola seafood market, **Joe Patti's Seafood at 524 S. B St.,** whose shrimp boats were involved in the filming of *Forrest Gump*. Photos of the film shoot are on a poster near the cash registers. Jackson has won two Georgia Author of the Year awards and is a *New York Times* and *USA Today* bestselling author. She now lives in Decatur, Georgia, but returns often to visit family in Pensacola. (See Destin, FL)

Using the pen name S. Usher Evans, Pensacolian Whitney Sanders writes young adult fantasy, adult fantasy and science fiction novels. A popular author at fan conventions across the country, Evans has written seventeen novels. Her book *City of Veils* won the Florida Young Adult Project Book of the Year in 2019. Her small independent press, Sun's Golden Ray Publishing, operates out of Pensacola. According to her bio, "Evans will talk about how great Pensacola, Florida, is to anyone who'll sit long enough."

Alabama native and Pensacola resident Katherine Clark is well known for sitting hours on end, interviewing, and transcribing oral biographies. Her most recent one is *My Exaggerated Life: Pat Conroy as told to Katherine Clark*. She has authored four novels in her *Mountain Brook* series. She received the 2015 Willie Morris Award for Southern Fiction for *The Headmaster's Darlings: A Mountain Brook Novel*, set in Birmingham, Alabama. Clark also won accolades for the book *Milking the Moon: Eugene Walter as Told to Katherine Clark*. (See Mobile, AL)

Alex Kava, a *New York Times* bestselling author who divides her time

TURN ON THE HEADLIGHTS IN FLORIDA

If it's rainy, foggy, or misty, turn on the vehicle lights in Florida. By law, anytime the windshield wipers are in use (rain), or in conditions of fog, smoke, or mist, even if the sun is shining, headlamps are required on all vehicles.

ROARING '20s ROAD TRIP
along the Old Spanish Trail

The name Old Spanish Trail conjures up visions of Spanish conquistadors herding cattle, slashing through palmettos, and staking claims for Spain. Not to be confused with the cattle trail by the same name, this Old Spanish Trail is one of the earliest auto-touring roads in America.

In 1915, 400 people, including mayors and businessmen, gathered at the Battle House Hotel in Mobile (AL) and envisioned a tourism concept that would capture America's heart. Their plan was to develop one continuous paved road to connect the southern states. The idea grew to stretch across the continent from St. Augustine (FL) to San Diego (CA). It was completed by 1929 with milestones at the beginning, middle and end – and a few more along the way.

In a time before highways were numbered, imagine riding in a touring car like the Model T, rumbling from town to town following the Old Spanish Trail touring map to see the historical sites along the southern border of the country. Bridges, like the one that replaced the ferry over Mobile Bay, were built to complete the Old Spanish Trail. Tourist stops, trail depots, markers, and Old Spanish Trail placards picturing a conquistador appeared along the route.

Cities and towns (mentioned in this book) where the Old Spanish Trail passed include Bay St. Louis, Pass Christian, Gulfport, Biloxi, Ocean Springs, Gautier, Pascagoula, Moss Point in Mississippi; Mobile, Robertsdale, St. Elmo in Alabama; and Pensacola, Milton, Crestview, and DeFuniak Springs in Florida. Many of these towns still have streets named Old Spanish Trail. Though the original roadway was bypassed or realigned by Highway 90 in the east and Highway 80 in the west, vestiges of it are still visible in parts of Florida, including Milton in the Panhandle.

between Florida and Nebraska, has been honored by both states for her writing achievement. The novel *Stranded*, part of her *Maggie O'Dell* detective series, was a 2013 Florida Book Award bronze winner and the 2014 Nebraska Book Award winner. Kava, who winters near Pensacola in her home in Santa Rosa County, has written more than twenty novels and been published in over thirty-five countries. According to an interview with Philip K. Jason for *Florida Weekly*, Kava bought her home on Blackwater Bay in Santa Rosa County in 2004 just before Hurricane Ivan hit the area. The following year Hurricane Dennis hit. Kava uses her first-hand experience of those hurricanes and Pensacola Beach in *Damaged*, book eight of her *Maggie O'Dell* series. Her personal knowledge of the nearby town of Milton, the Blackwater River, and the Blackwater State Park is evident in the Ryder Creed series. In *Lost Creed*, the fourth in the *Creed* series, characters O' Dell, an FBI profiler, and Creed, a former Marine turned K-9 trainer, work together. In the novel, Kava effectively uses both her home states, Nebraska and Florida, as locations for the human trafficking plot. The Florida Panhandle is home to Creed's fictional search-scent dog training facility. Among the actual Florida settings in *Lost Creed*, Kava includes **Garcon Point**, a tip of land which separates Escambia Bay and Blackwater Bay; the **Yellow River Marsh Preserve State Park, Dickerson City Rd. at Garcon Point Rd. (CR-191) Milton;** and the nearby **Waffle House** at **2662 Avalon Blvd., Milton.** The book won the 2019 Nebraska Book Award.

Pensacola is part of the settings for three other of Kava's books: *Whitewash, Exposed,* and *A Necessary Evil.* In *Breaking Creed*, Ryder Creed hangs out at a rundown café on Pensacola Beach, which stands in the shadows of the towering **Margaritaville Hotel at 165 Fort Pickens Rd**. Jimmy Buffett, songwriter and author, bought, completed, and opened the hotel in 2010 when the developers abandoned the project due to the BP Oil Spill. Locals sing Buffett's praises for helping out when times were bad. It was the first of the Margaritaville Hotels but rebranded in 2023 as Pensacola Beach Resort. As a boy growing up in Alabama, Buffett spent many summer days on Pensacola Beach.

Pensacola native Craig Pittman has written several books but gets the most laughs from *Oh Florida! How America's Weirdest State Influences the Rest of the Nation.* That 2016 Florida Book Award winner is also a *New York Times* bestseller. As a writer for the *Tampa Bay Times,* Pittman earned a stellar reputation as an environmental journalist, writing books about manatees and panthers, and scores of magazine and newspaper articles about the environment. He has won at least six top Florida investigative environmental journalism awards. In 2020 he was named a Florida Book Heritage Festival "Literary Legend." *Flamingo Magazine* listed his 2020 book *Cat Tale: The Wild, Weird Battle to Save the Florida Panther* as one of twenty-four books every Floridian should have. His 2010 book *Manatee Insanity: Inside the War Over Florida's Most Famous Endangered Species* was named one of twenty-one essential books for Floridians by the Florida Humanities Council. Pittman grew up in an area of Pensacola where **University Town Plaza** is now located and attended **Pensacola Christian School (10 Brent Ln.).**

A husband-and-wife team blended the benchmarks of the city — history, naval aviation, the ocean, and music — and took their work on the road. Pensacola physician Jack Fleming (1924-2019) and wife Carolyn (1926-2019) wrote the book and lyrics for *Seaplane!*, an "all-American family musical." The show celebrates Glenn Curtiss as the father of naval aviation and showcases Pensacola as the cradle of aviation. The musical opened in 1989 in Pensacola and

went on to Washington, D.C. for a special performance at the Kennedy Center the next year. From 1992-1994, the show ran in summer stock in Hammondsport, New York, the second setting for the story. The last production of the original show was in Pensacola in 1994. In 2015 the show enjoyed a revival at Pensacola's **Saenger Theatre, 118 S. Palafox,** in celebration of the 100th birthday of Naval Air Station-Pensacola.

Pensacola's Saenger Theatre opened in 1925 and boasts a rich history of showing vaudeville acts, silent films, and Broadway shows. Pensacola's husband and wife team Jack and Carolyn Fleming staged their musical *Seaplane!* at The Saenger before it went on to The Kennedy Center.

Gulf Islands National Seashore protects two sections on Pensacola Beach, one at Fort Pickens and the other east of Portofino to Navarre. Earle Bowden's book *Gulf Islands: The Sands of All Time: Preserving America's Largest National Seashore* recounts the efforts to protect this seashore.

Named after a writer, J. Earle Bowden Way is a seven-mile road that connects Pensacola Beach and Navarre in the Gulf Islands National Seashore, an appropriate tribute to the writer called the "Father of the Gulf Islands National Seashore" for his continual efforts to preserve the natural beauty of the area. The leisurely drive provides a magnificent and breathtaking view of pristine nature, where the sea meets the shore. Occasionally in heavy rains or hurricane season, the road may be temporarily closed since it's so close to the water.

When UFO chronicler Ed Walters moved out of his home at 612 Silverthorn in Gulf Breeze, a model UFO resembling the UFO he had photographed was discovered in the attic. The model is now property of the University of West Florida Historic Trust and on display at UFO's Pensacola Beach.

UFO's miniature golf on Pensacola Beach pays homage to the area's reputation as a UFO hot spot. The mini-golf course is accented with alien mannequins and bright neon lights. Inside the ticket office are displays of a Styrofoam spaceship model and framed newspaper articles about the Gulf Breeze sightings.

GULF BREEZE, FLORIDA

Gulf Breeze sits three miles across Pensacola Bay from Pensacola and provides the only highway access to Pensacola Beach from the west. Once a breezy getaway dotted with cozy cottages for Pensacola residents to escape the heat, friendly neighborhoods now welcome fulltime residents. Though a relatively new town, incorporated in 1961, shady, mid-century modern neighborhoods mixed with bungalows and million-dollar houses paint a charming suburban picture. With piers and beaches facing the Sound, Gulf Breeze also provides the land entrance to the Naval Live Oaks recreational portion of the Gulf Islands National Seashore.

Gulf Breeze's best claim to literary fame is allegedly one of the greatest hoaxes ever pulled in the Unidentified Flying Objects culture. In 1987, when local builder Ed Walters gained international attention for his UFO sightings, tourists and residents flocked to **Shoreline Park in Gulf Breeze** and other spots nearby to search the skies for UFOs. Walters' nearly one hundred UFO sightings and Polaroid photographs sparked a cottage industry of publishing and a media frenzy. Walters (with then-wife Frances) wrote three books, *The*

Shoreline Park at 800 Shoreline Drive in Gulf Breeze overlooks the Sound and provides a clear view of the skies. During the 1990s, the park was a hot spot for UFO sightings. It's still the best place to see fireworks on the Fourth of July.

Gulf Breeze Sightings, UFO Abductions in Gulf Breeze, and *UFOs Are Real: Here's the Proof.* In pure Florida tourism fashion, Gulf Breeze and the surrounding towns named a bar and a used car lot with UFO terms like Area 51. Restaurants added extraterrestrial items like UFO sundaes to the menus, and entrepreneurs sold T-shirts with designs depicting aliens on the beach.

The area even hosted international UFO symposiums at Pensacola Beach hotels. Local singer Ken Manning's music video *Gulf Breeze* won one of the state's film and motion picture association's top awards in 1999. After Ed Walters moved out of his home at **612 Silverthorn** in Gulf Breeze, a tiny model UFO rsembling the UFO he claimed to have photographed was discovered in the attic and in 1990 a witness, using only his first name, told Gulf Breeze officials he had been present during the UFO fake-photo session. He later recanted his statement.

But locals love the lore. In the summer of 2020, a Pensacola Beach hotel group revamped its miniature golf course using a UFO and alien space theme. The 18-hole mini-golf course, now named UFO's, is a humorous tribute to the sightings complete with alien mannequins. Inside, they feature a display of *Gulf Breeze Sentinel* newspapers and the Styrofoam model of a UFO, used in the alleged hoax. In the 1980s, when locals aware of Walters' UFO sightings drove along U. S. Highway 98 through the Naval Live Oaks, part of the Gulf Islands National Seashore, it was common to spot strange lights and shapes in the pitch-black skies. Even now along that stretch at night, drivers look up to the dark skies, wondering.

Strange flying objects, Gulf Breeze, and Highway 98 also appear in Leslie Wolfe's first novel, *Executive* (2011). In the thriller, an Air Force drone flying out of fictional Mackenzie Airfield goes astray and causes a deadly accident on Highway 98 near Gulf Breeze. Though most of the book's action takes place in California, the main character, Alex Hoffmann, comes to the Florida Panhandle to investigate the drone disaster. Wolfe, a bestselling author, has written five Alex Hoffmann novels, three other series, a screenplay, and two standalone novels. Wolfe lives in Santa Rosa County and confesses to being inspired by the geography of her Florida region. Her genres include thrillers, crime fiction, detective novels, and technology thrillers, all extensively researched.

Jeannie O. Zokan, author of two award-winning novels, *Existence of Pity* (2015) and *Courage Without Grace* (2021), writes from her home in Gulf Breeze, ten minutes from the beach. Though her recent books are women's fiction, she also writes science fiction.

NAVARRE, FLORIDA

The legend woven around the founding of Navarre could almost be a romance novel. Dashing Army officer Guy Wyman fell in love with a French nurse during World War I and wanted to marry her. At the time, immigration laws made it illegal for her to come to the U.S. as either his fiancée or his wife. So, Guy legally adopted her as his child and brought her to the beach settlement once known as Eagan. He then founded Navarre. Though the story reads like fiction, it is a fact that Navarre Beach is a relaxing place to escape and has the longest fishing pier in the Gulf of Mexico — 1,545-feet long.

To see **Navarre Beach, take the scenic route from Pensacola Beach, and drive east along Bowden Way (the two-lane beach access road)** to witness the breathtaking views of the Emerald Coast, with the Gulf of Mexico on the south and the Intercoastal Waterway on the north. **Pass through the Gulf Islands National Seashore and continue to the end of the road.** To return to Highway 98, cross over the **Navarre Beach Causeway** to the north; it deadends at Highway 98. Navarre Beach, part of the Gulf Islands National

BE ON THE LOOKOUT
Joe Exotic of *Tiger King* fame was arrested in Gulf Breeze.
Serial killer Ted Bundy was captured in Pensacola.

Seashore, offers four miles of pristine beaches open to the public.

Former Navarre resident, author Lenora Nazworth writing as Lenora Worth, has written more than eighty contemporary romance and suspense novels and is a *New York Times, USA Today,* and *Publishers' Weekly* bestselling author. With over three million books in print including popular Amish novels, Worth still finds time to sign books at literary events, give a keynote speech at a book fair or participate as a faculty member for area writing conferences. Worth's Southern stories are often set in Florida or Georgia, where she was born. She collaborated with Marilyn Turk of Niceville for a two-author Christmas collection featuring landmarks in the literary rich setting of DeFuniak Springs. (See Niceville, FL and DeFuniak Springs, FL)

DESTIN AND NICEVILLE, FLORIDA

Whether the official slogan is "Florida's Most Relaxing Place" or "Florida's Best Kept Secret," Navarre Beach provides an eastern gateway to the Gulf Islands National Seashore. According author Jeannie Zokan, a former Navarre resident now living in Gulf Breeze, Navarre's pristine Opal Beach was created in 1995 when Hurricane Opal flattened the dunes.

This former sleepy fishing village of Destin welcomes more than 3.6 million visitors annually, but with a resident population of a little over 14,000, the area is more popular for its book settings than as a home to authors. Writers visit here, but others prefer living across the bridge in Niceville.

Murder Makes Waves, number four in the eight book *Southern Sisters* series by Anne George (1927-2001), takes place at a beachfront condo in Destin. When the body of a new friend washes up on the beach, the two sisters attempt to solve the crime. The author, an Alabama native, was Alabama's state poet and nominated for a Pulitzer in poetry. But it was the humorous cozy mysteries that garnered George her greatest fan base and an Agatha Award for literary achievement.

Bestselling author Joshilyn Jackson's novel *Never Have I Ever* features a protagonist who uses diving as therapy. When researching for her novel, Jackson learned to dive at Emerald Coast Scuba in Destin. In the acknowledgments in *Never Have I Ever*, Jackson also credits the divers with helping her scout and invent submerged locations, as well as diving terminology and technicalities. **Emerald Coast Scuba** is located at **503B Harbor Blvd.** (See Pensacola, FL)

Cozy mystery writer Sherry Harris' popular *Chloe Jackson Sea Glass Saloon Mystery* series features Destin locations. Harris often vacationed with her parents in Destin, where her parents later moved. She continues to visit since her mother still lives in Destin. (See Scenic 30A, FL)

Though not a resident of Destin, Vicki Hinze, a New Orleans native and *USA Today* bestselling author, lives across the bridge in Niceville. She has written four nonfiction books and more than forty novels. She writes military romance and military suspense along with genre-blending works and Christian fiction. She has written nine series, also writing under the pseudonyms Victoria Barrett and Victoria Cole. Many of her works feature the Destin area. With seventeen military novels to her credit, nearby Eglin Air Force Base, no doubt, serves as both inspiration and a reliable resource for her work.

Eglin Air Force Base is home to the **Air Force Armament Museum (100 Museum Dr.).** Jimmy Doolittle's raiders practiced at Eglin Air Field before the Tokyo Raid in 1942. Founder of the gonzo journalism movement, Hunter S. Thompson got his start writing for the Eglin Air Force Base newspaper *The Command Courier* while stationed there in 1957. He lied about his experience and got the job writing sports and traveling the country covering the Eglin football team. He broke base policy by also writing for *The Playground News* in Fort Walton Beach. To date there is no museum exhibit about Thompson.

Linda Sealy Knowles, an Alabama native who lives in Niceville, penned her first novel when she retired to Florida. A prolific writer, she writes historical romance westerns and has finished more than a dozen so far in her busy retirement.

Marilyn Turk, who also lives in Niceville, writes for magazines and pens Christian suspense novels. Her most recent is a four-book *Coastal Lights Legacy* series set in the South. The fourth book in the series, *Rekindled Light*, features the Pensacola Lighthouse located at the Naval Air Station in Pensacola. A lighthouse enthusiast, she spent time living in one with her husband as a voluntary caretaker at the Little River Lighthouse off the coast of Cutler, Maine. Her interest often manifests itself with a lighthouse setting or theme in her work. She is director of Blue Lakes Christian Writers Retreat in Andalusia, Alabama. Her 2021 novel *Not My Party* is also set in the Panhandle. (See Pensacola, FL)

The Pensacola Lighthouse is featured in Marilyn Turk's historical novel, *Rekindled Light*. Turk calls herself a literary archaeologist and builds plots around stories in history. In *Rekindled Light*, a Union officer finds the Pensacola lighthouse lens removed by Confederates during the Civil War. The officer is also in charge of construction of the lighthouse keeper's house, as seen in the photo.

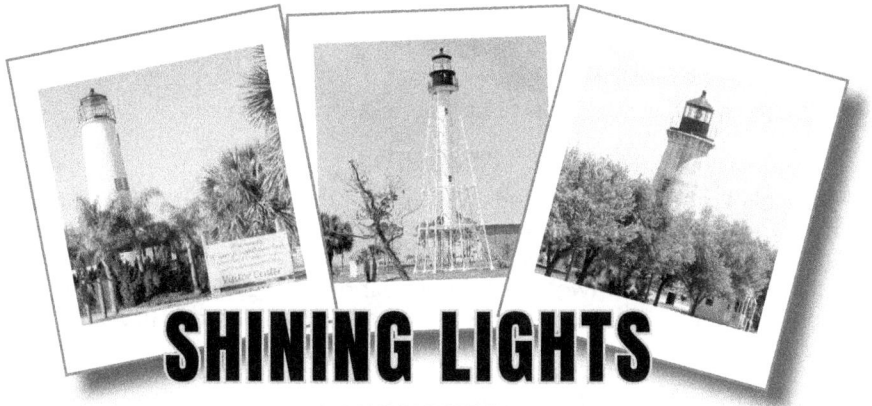

SHINING LIGHTS

MISSISSIPPI

Biloxi Lighthouse – Located in the median of U.S. Highway 90 at Porter Avenue, the Biloxi "light" is one of the oldest surviving lighthouses and an icon of the City of Biloxi. Built in 1848, the cast-iron lighthouse represents a beacon of strength and survival to the community. It has survived dozens of hurricanes including Camille and Katrina. It was operated continually by the government for 100 years and is now privately operated. It is decorated for holidays and open for morning tours.

Gulfport Lighthouse – This replica of the Ship Island Lighthouse destroyed in Hurricane Katrina was erected in 2011 at Jones Park, Gulfport Municipal Marina, US-90 (Beach Blvd. at Hwy. 49). The lighthouse replica is decorated for the Christmas holidays and the centerpiece of the Gulfport Harbor Lights Festival, the largest Christmas light display in the state. No inside tours are available.

Pascagoula Lighthouse – When Hurricane George toppled the lighthouse on Round Island, four miles off the coast, and reconstruction efforts were disrupted by Hurricane Katrina, portions of the lighthouse were transported to the safety of Pascagoula, restored and reassembled. It is the namesake of Lighthouse Park on the east bank of the Pascagoula River on Hwy. 90 near the foot of the bridge; it's open for tours on a limited schedule.

ALABAMA

Middle Bay Lighthouse – Located in Mobile Bay, this hexagonal-shaped, Chesapeake Bay-style lighthouse dates to 1885 and is listed on the National Register of Historic Places. It can be seen from The Grand Hotel in Point Clear and from Fairhope on a clear day (bring good binoculars). It ceased operation in 1967 and is not open for tours. It has been renovated and boasts a solar-powered red light.

Sand Island – Three miles off the coast from Dauphin Island at the mouth of Mobile Bay, this lighthouse stands on tiny Sand Island and is disappearing. It can be seen from Fort Morgan on a clear day and is only accessible by boat. There's been a lighthouse on this island since 1835. The current one dates to 1864. The City of Dauphin Island has attempted dredging and restoration of the eroding island, but their efforts were foiled by Hurricane Isaac in 2011. The 400 acres on which the lighthouse originally stood now numbers less than 15 acres.

FLORIDA

Pensacola Lighthouse – Erected 1859, the lighthouse is open to the public and offers special events like ghost tours and Blue Angels viewings. But the 177-step climb up the spiraling ironwork staircase is a queasy one. From the top visitors can see three counties and two states. On a clear night, the light can be seen for 27 miles. The lighthouse is located on a bluff overlooking Pensacola Bay at Pensacola Naval Air Base near the Naval Aviation Museum.

Cape San Blas Lighthouse – This historic iron lighthouse was relocated inland to Core Park at Port St. Joe and opened to the public in 2014. The "skeletal" type light had originally been located on a "cape" that jutted out in the Gulf of Mexico near the St. Joseph peninsula. It is listed on the National Register of Historic Places. The park has several historic lighthouse buildings; the lighthouse is open for climbing.

St. George Island Lighthouse and Museum – Located near Eastpoint, across the bridge from Apalachicola, this stone and brick conical lighthouse is open to the public. Dating to 1852, Hurricane Opal caused the lighthouse to lean in 1995, and Hurricane Wilma knocked it over in 2005. Lighthouse aficionados from across the Gulf Coast region gathered to put the historic structure back together. Volunteers salvaged, cleaned, and reassembled what is now the centerpiece of Lighthouse Park. There's also a museum.

SOUNDS AND VIEWS

The Gulf Intracoastal Waterway, where the big ships travel, runs 1050 miles from Carrabelle (FL) near Apalachicola all the way to Texas passing through ports at Apalachicola, Panama City, Pensacola, Mobile, Pascagoula, and Gulfport. Locals call it "the Sound."

Bay St. Louis sits at the Bay of Saint Louis and the Mississippi Sound, which opens into the Gulf of Mexico.

The Mississippi Coast faces the Mississippi Sound, not the Gulf of Mexico.

Mobile, Alabama, is on Mobile Bay, not the Gulf of Mexico.

Pensacola, Florida, faces Pensacola Bay.

Pensacola Beach is flanked by the Intracoastal Waterway (the Sound) and the Gulf of Mexico.

Apalachicola faces Apalachicola Bay, not the Gulf of Mexico.

There's not an ocean in sight.

The Beaches of South Walton (Walton County, FL) are located primarily along Scenic Highway 30A, off Highway 98. Public access is provided with boardwalks leading to sugar white sands and turquoise waters.

SCENIC 30A, FLORIDA

This twenty-six-mile stretch that hugs the coastline features modern, yet quaint, seaside villages reminiscent of Old Florida. The hub of the stretch is Seaside, with its bustling Sundog Books, popular eateries, and sidewalks leading to beach-style cottages with front porches and picket fences. The town showcases New Urbanism architecture. Many of the other communities along the scenic highway are also part of the master plan devised in the 1970s. Scenic 30A is now credited with revitalizing the architectural style of urbanism.

In *The Forgotten*, bestselling author David Baldacci's main character approaches this part of Florida from the northeast and circles around Choctawhatchee Bay. Somewhere along this stretch Baldacci places his fictional town of Paradise. The book's principal character Army Special Agent John Puller travels south along Highway 85 and passes by real places like Shalimar, Cinco Bayou, and Fort Walton Beach. He continues along the Miracle Strip Parkway (Hwy.98), passes the real Eglin Air Force Base, zooms across the real bridge, drives through the real Destin, and shortly thereafter arrives in the fictional town of Paradise. Even though this description accurately sets the geographical stage, some locals doubt Baldacci ever visited the Florida Panhandle. Baldacci captured the heat, sugar sand, and emerald waters correctly, but some say his descriptions describe South Florida better than the Emerald Coast.

Independent author Deborah Rine is more specific with the setting of her *Emerald Coast Mystery* series. All six novels include Scenic Highway 30A in the title, starting with *The Girl on 30A* and *Envy on 30A*, both published

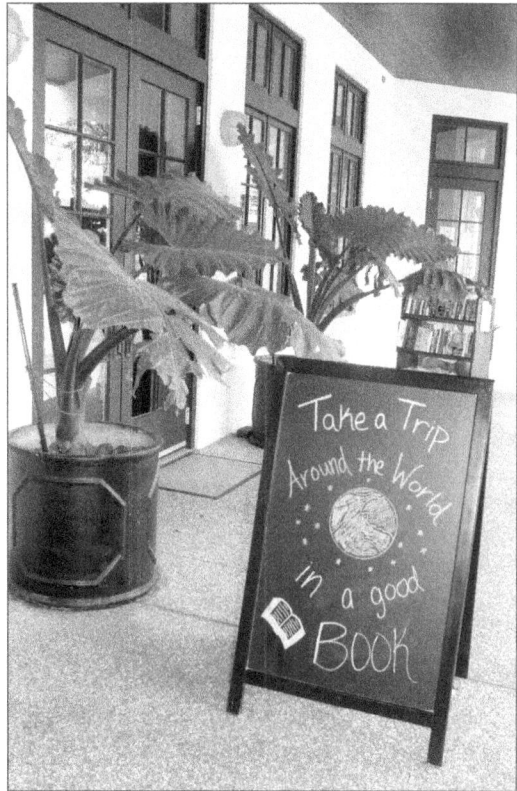

Rosemary Beach offers posh condominiums, exclusive shopping opportunities, gourmet restaurants, coffee shops, and Hidden Lantern Books. Designed in 1995 and one of three planned communities on the east end of Scenic 30A, Rosemary Beach realtors listed houses for a median price of $1.3 million in 2022. Deborah Rine's novels feature a realtor as the protagonist.

in 2018, and continuing with *Missing on 30A* in 2020, *Double Trouble on 30A* and *Riptide on 30A* in 2022, and *Blue on 30A* in 2023. Rine, who grew up in Illinois and lived in Sweden, Belgium, France, and Italy, chose to retire in Freeport in Walton County after vacationing for years on the Emerald Coast. She now lives just miles from where her books are set.

Rine's *Emerald Coast Mystery* series includes mention of almost all the beaches plus many restaurants and shops. In *Missing on 30A*, the protagonist is a realtor with access to multi-million-dollar beach homes and developments along 30A. The character brings the reader along on her beach runs beginning at Grayton Beach, and then on visits to spas and yoga studios. Most of the restaurants and shops in the book exist, while some are fictional. Clues for solving the murder also take the reader to Panama City and St. Andrew's Marina.

Sherry Harris' popular *Chloe Jackson Sea Glass Saloon Mystery* series is set in Emerald Cove, a fictional beach town fifty miles west of Panama City, fifty miles east of Pensacola, next door to Destin, and west of Grayton Beach in Walton County. A cartographer would pinpoint the spot on Scenic Highway 30A. Harris loves writing about the area and knows it well. She first visited Destin the 1980s, her parents moved there in 1991, and her mother still lives in Destin. Harris' husband was stationed at Hurlburt Field, and they lived in the Panhandle community of Shalimar from 2000 to 2003.

Harris, who now lives in Northern Virginia, is the former international president of Sisters in Crime writer's organization. Her readers get a good taste of the Destin area when reading the first book in the series, *From Beer to Eternity*. Protagonist Chloe Jackson attempts to solve a murder by visiting local tourist sites and in doing so reveals much of the history of the area. The book mentions numerous Destin locations including **McGuire's Irish Pub at 33 U.S. Hwy. 98** across from **Destin Harbor; Emerald Grande Resort Hotel in Harborwalk Village, Destin Harbor; Crab Trap Restaurant, 3500 Scenic Hwy. 98 in James Lee Park; Okaloosa Island Bridge; the East Pass Bridge;** and **Gulfarium at 1010 Miracle Strip Pkwy. (Hwy. 98), Fort Walton Beach.**

SANTA ROSA BEACH, FLORIDA

Santa Rosa Beach is one of sixteen neighborhoods along Scenic 30A in South Walton County. To many passersby, these communities seem to flow seamlessly and beautifully together. Tourist information, however, says each has a distinct personality.

Sean Dietrich, known to his followers as Sean of the South, is a popular podcaster, blogger, humorist, and author who was transplanted in Walton County at age fourteen. He once typed rough drafts on a typewriter from a trailer, parked across the yard from his house in Santa Rosa Beach, not quite a mile from Choctawhatchee Bay.

Lately he writes of moving to Alabama because of the increase in population in the Florida Panhandle. Dietrich writes a daily blog with over 100,000 followers and is a frequent contributor to Southern magazines. He's written more than a dozen books. His mystery, *The Other Side of the Bay*, is set in the Florida Panhandle.

Old Florida-style cottages still stand in Grayton Beach, though they are quickly disappearing. Sprawling oaks provide shade for yards enclosed with white picket fences.

Grayton Beach is an artsy beach town with quirky murals and an absence of modern commercialism evident in other towns along Scenic 30A.

GRAYTON BEACH, FLORIDA

This quaint, historic village, founded in 1890 seems to showcase the last remnants of Old Florida. The town, near the 2000-acre Grayton Beach State Park, is one of the earliest settlements in the area. The hamlet boasts a funky atmosphere and the unofficial slogan of "Nice Dogs, Strange People."

Jill Sanders, a *USA Today, New York Times,* and international bestselling contemporary romance author has written more than sixty books and eleven series, several which take place along the Emerald Coast. The Grayton series is a seven-book collection set in the fictional beach town, Surf Breeze, which sounds a lot like Grayton Beach looks. In *The Last Resort,* main character Cassey is transforming a neglected family-owned property into the Boardwalk Bar & Grill. The family name – Grayton. Though the author lives across Choctawhatchee Bay in nearby Freeport, she enjoys walking the beach and watching the sunsets at **Grayton Beach State Park.** In 2020, Grayton Beach was named the best beach in the U.S. by Stephen "Dr. Beach" Leatherman, a coastal scientist and college professor.

WATERCOLOR, FLORIDA

New York Times bestselling, award-winning author Karen White (1964 -) is a part-time resident of WaterColor, spending the rest of her year in her native Georgia. Author of more than twenty books, she writes in several genres including Southern women's fiction, contemporary paranormal fiction, historical romance, and women's detective fiction. All her books are set in the South and feature Southern female protagonists. As a child, White was inspired by Northwest Florida, often visiting her grandparents who lived in nearby De-Funiak Springs. *Flight Patterns* is set in Apalachicola, while *The Beach Trees* is set in Katrina-ravaged Biloxi. (See Biloxi, MS and Apalachicola, FL)

SEASIDE, FLORIDA

If you've seen the Jim Carrey movie *The Truman Show,* you've seen Seaside and its quaint Florida cottages with rose-covered picket fences, bicycling paths, footpaths, shady sidewalks, and cobblestone streets. The movie, filmed in 1998 in this master-planned community, is based on a speculative science fiction script by Andrew Niccol (1964 -) about a utopian community. In the town, all the characters' actions are scripted in a reality show – except for those of Truman Burbank, the main character. **The Truman House** from the film, now a private residence, is located at **31 Natchez St**. Though the story was never a book, Niccol did publish *The Truman Show: The Shooting Script.* The movie won an Oscar and a BAFTA for best original screenplay, three Golden Globes, and made the town of Seaside famous with moviegoers worldwide.

Writers come to Seaside for another reason. Since 2013 authors, editors, poets, critics, agents, and readers have been traveling to Seaside to learn and write. What began as the Seaside Writers Conference has evolved into the week-long Longleaf Writers Conference featuring top names in the literary world. While attendees once stayed in Katrina Cottages transported from the Mississippi Coast, they now stay in local housing while awaiting the completion of a new academic village. Seminars, round tables, and workshops are held at the **Seaside Institute Assembly Hall, 168 Smolian Circle,** while plenty of writers hang out at bustling **Sundog Books, 869 Central Square**. Conference attire is casual, flip flops welcome. Organizers offer fellowships and scholarships and showcase popular fiction and creative nonfiction writers and poets.

New Urbanism architecture is the hallmark of Seaside. The town square, which is more of a horseshoe shape than a square, is the site of festivals, food trucks, dog walkers, and people watchers. The "square" is flanked with shops, restaurants, and the popular Sundog Books

ROSEMARY BEACH, FLORIDA

Young adult and romance author Abbi Glines has written an entire series, fourteen to date, named after this planned community with a population of around 4300. *The Rosemary Beach* series is one of her most popular. Glines, a Birmingham, Alabama native, is on *New York Times*, *USA Today*, and *The Wall Street Journal* bestseller lists, and now lives in New Hampshire.

You may find a copy of one of her books at the **The Hidden Lantern at 84 North Barrett Square**, a bustling shopping area. Travelers to this resort town can book a modern vacation rental in a million-dollar property in Tabby Lofts, right above the bookshop. Rosemary Beach offers upscale shops and eateries reflective of those described in Deborah Rine's *Emerald Coast Mystery* series. Her main character, a former saleswoman for expensive leather handbags, becomes a multi-million-dollar real estate agent and frequents wine bars, coffee shops and Tripadvisor's top two ranked restaurants, **Restaurant Pardis** in **Barrett Square** and **LaCrema Tapas and Chocolate, 38 Main St.**

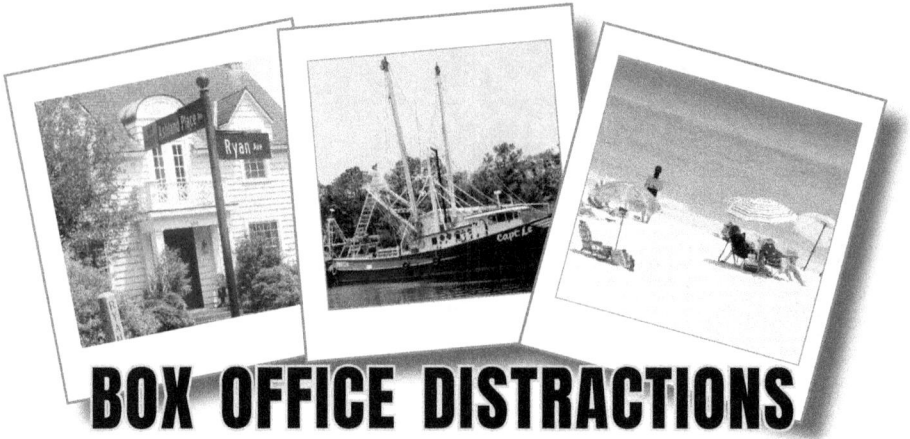

BOX OFFICE DISTRACTIONS

BAY ST. LOUIS (MS)

This Property Is Condemned (1966) starring Robert Redford and Natalie Wood was filmed in Bay St. Louis. Despite major hurricane damages to other parts of town, tourists can still take a movie location walking tour, beginning at the **Bay St. Louis Depot**, the current visitor's center and depot used in the movie.

GULFPORT (MS)

The delightful romantic comedy *Christmas in Mississippi* (2017 made for TV) was shot almost entirely in Gulfport. You can grab a *Coastal Mississippi Guide* and visit movie locations like **Fishbone Alley, Triplett-Day Drugstore,** restaurants, and the **Island View Casino Resort.** In December visitors can enjoy the million-plus Christmas lights at **Jones Park** on the beach for the Gulfport Harbor Lights Winter Festival – just like in the movie.

BILOXI (MS)

Biloxi Blues (1988) was set in **Keesler Air Force Base**, Biloxi, but filmed entirely in Arkansas.

PASCAGOULA-GAUTIER (MS)

Stone Cold (1991) has plenty of scenes filmed in Bay St. Louis, Gautier, Pascagoula, Mobile, and Pensacola. The big budget action film about bikers was the first film for Brian Bosworth ("The Boz") in a Razzie-nominated performance. Actors from Mississippi high schools helped round out the cast.

MOBILE-FAIRHOPE (AL)

For Stephen Spielberg's box office hit, *Close Encounters of the Third Kind* (1977), Mobile school children dressed in gray alien costumes and masks acting as extras for the film. Much of the movie was shot in the Mobile area — in residential neighborhoods, at **Mobile Civic Center**, and old **Brookley Air Force Base**, now an industrial complex.

MOBILE-FAIRHOPE (AL)

Jordan Peele's Oscar-winning horror movie *Get Out* (2017) was filmed in Fairhope and Mobile, with scenes on Mobile Bay. To see where the majority of the action was filmed, drive by **6892 Heathcroft Lane** in **Fairhope** or **Barton Academy** at **504 Government St.** in **Mobile**. The opening scene was filmed at **Ryan and DeLeon Streets** in the **Ashland Place Historic District** neighborhood.

BAYOU LA BATRE (AL)

Forrest Gump (1994) The Bubba Gump Shrimp Co., owned by Lt. Dan in the Oscar-winning movie, was set in Bayou La Batre but filmed in South Carolina. The restaurant chain by the same name and inspired by the movie began in California. Somehow shrimp boats from Joe Patti's Seafood in Pensacola were on location.

PENSACOLA TO DESTIN (FL)

Jaws II (1978) was set in fictional Amity Island with most of the movie shot at Pensacola Beach, Fort Pickens, Navarre, Oklaloosa Island, and Destin, with plenty of Gulf Breeze High School students as extras.

SEASIDE (FL)

The Truman Show (1998) Actor Jim Carrey's life is a reality show in this popular movie filmed in the perfectly planned community of Seaside. You can visit the clock tower, market, drugstore, post office and walk beside cottages with picket fences and climbing roses for a complete film immersion experience – and it's real. People live there!

WEWAHITCHKA (FL)

Ulee's Gold (1997) starring Peter Fonda as a beekeeper was set and filmed in the swamps and town of Wewahitchka. You can still buy **Lanier Honey** from the family who offered their property and expertise for the film.

DeFuniak Springs

Dozens of Victorian homes, a library, an assembly hall, churches, and a wooded park still encircle the picturesque, perfectly round Lake DeFuniak where row boats once ferried lovers of the written and spoken word to the evening readings and lectures of "Chautauqua."

In historic DeFuniak Springs, forty of the town's 200 historic buildings are listed on the National Register of Historic Places. About an hour's drive east of Pensacola along I-10 or thirty minutes north of Scenic Highway 30A and the towns of Seaside and Santa Rosa Beach, this town features several important literary sights and the oldest continually operating library in the State of Florida. It's a side trip worthy of several hours. A good place to begin is the depot at **1140 Circle Dr.,** for information on the walking (or driving) tour. Placards have been installed at places of interest. But for some, just looking at the gorgeous homes is satisfying enough.

Popular writers who visited DeFuniak Springs for Chautauqua events included Harriet Beecher Stowe, author of *Uncle Tom's Cabin*; Julia Ward Howe, the poet best known for writing "The Battle Hymn of the Republic;" and Cincinnatus Heine Miller, Poet of the Sierras, who wrote under the pen name Joaquin Miller. Two notable writers, however, lived on the premises of the culturally-minded community.

Dream Cottage, 404 Circle Dr., was the home of Wallace Bruce (1844-1914). The Yale graduate was an early president of the DeFuniak Chautauqua and an established poet who once served as Poet Laureate of the Masonic Lodge of Canongate of Kilwinning, Scotland. He would deliver poetry, especially his major poem "Parson Allen's Ride," to audiences. From 1874 to the 1890s he also published *The Land of Burns, The Yosemite, The Hudson Highlands, From the Hudson to the Yosemite, Old Homestead Poems,* and *Wayside Poems. Harper's Weekly* and *Blackwood Magazine* also published his works.

Isabella MacDonald Alden (1841-1930), writing under the pen name Pansy, lived in **Pansy Cottage, 392 Circle Dr.** She wrote over 100 children's books beginning in 1865 with *Helen Lester* to 1931 with her posthumously published memoir *Memories of Yesteryear*. She was immensely popular during her time selling as many as 100,000 books annually, with copies translated into several languages. She co-edited a children's magazine, *Pansy*, with her husband G. R. Alden, a pastor. Her Christian faith books for young female readers, including the intriguing title *Four Girls at Chautauqua*, are still available in print and electronically.

The **DeFuniak Library, 3 Circle Dr.,** opened on December 20, 1887, and has never closed. Even when Chautauqua assemblies ended in 1928, the library continued to welcome readers. It is now part of the Walton County Public Library System. Author Harper Lee, who was friends with the librarian, presented a signed, first edition of *To Kill a Mockingbird* to the library. For years, the book was in circulation to library patrons, but now it's under glass for safekeeping. Visitors may ask to view it. Upon request, librarians will also play the magnificent antique Regina Music Box. Adjacent to the library is the Library Reading Garden with a lovely view of the lake.

LITTLE HOUSE IN THE WILDWOOD

Sixteen miles north of DeFuniak Springs near Westville is a historic marker commemorating where Laura Ingalls Wilder, husband Almanzo, and daughter Rose lived in 1891 and 1892. They moved from Minnesota for Almanzo's health and lived with relatives for a little less than a year. Ironically, Laura's health couldn't tolerate the Florida humidity. Daughter Rose Wilder Lane's short story "Innocence," published by *Harper's* in 1922, won the O. Henry Award. It is based on that time in Florida. A noted journalist and travel writer, she helped her mother with editing and publishing the popular *Little House* children's books. The marker is located eighteen miles north, northwest of Westville on County Rd. 163, north of Mims Rd. in the Poplar Head community.

The beaches along Scenic 30A are located within and between sixteen beach neighbor-hoods along a 26-mile stretch. The small seaside towns range from quaint old Florida cottages to posh shopping meccas and luxurious condominiums. Returning to Highway 98, travelers head east to Panama City Beach and Panama City.

PANAMA CITY BEACH, PANAMA CITY

Panama City Beach and Panama City are neighbors — beach towns separated by a bay and connected by a bridge. Despite the similar names, the two towns have different histories and attractions. Panama City, ten miles east of Panama City Beach, traces its roots to Revolutionary days and has been called by a series of names including Floriopolis, Park Resort, and Harrison. Its final name is, indeed, associated with Panama, the Central American country, but in a roundabout way. During the American excitement over the opening of the Panama Canal, industrialists and developers realized a straight line could be drawn from Chicago, the railroad capital, to Panama, the country. That line ran directly through this Florida port town. Thus, the christening of a new name in true Florida development mode. Today it's a bustling city popular for both commerce and industry as well as fishing and tourism. **The Panama City Publishing Company Museum at 1134 Beck Ave.** in historic St. Andrews offers a look back at the town's history through writers and newspapers, plus displays of 100-year-old printing equipment.

Panama City Beach, however, is famous as the Spring Break Capital of the World thanks to 1990-era reality television. Local authorities are trying to change the rowdy college student reputation and return to the family friendly aspect of the 26-mile-long beachfront. Before 1990, Panama City Beach was a quiet place. Still only about 15,000 people call it home, but in the busy season, the daily population swells to 100,000 for a total of 4.5 million visitors a year, according to the city's website. Both Panama City and Panama City Beach offer inspiration for veteran and novice writers, especially when it comes to regional flavor and colorful settings. Two popular novels – Nancy Bartholomew's *The Miracle Strip* (1998) and Michael Lister's *Thunder Beach* (2010) are rich in local settings, some real, some fictional, and some destroyed by Hurricane Michael in 2018.

Nancy Bartholomew's "strip" novels about an exotic dancer who solves mysteries are set in Panama City. The first of the Sierra Lavotini novels is appropriately titled *The Miracle Strip*, after the tourism name for the stretch of beaches and towns including Panama City. The series evolved when Bartholomew entered a short story in a Mystery Writers of America contest requiring a Florida setting. The story won first place and started her writing career. She was familiar with the Panhandle after spending childhood summers vacationing in areas like Mexico Beach, then later at Grayton Beach. Her visits to Panama City increased when writing the series. Her research included ride-alongs with the local police and spending nights in cheap motels with her family to capture the atmosphere. The other catchy series titles, all set in Panama City, include *Strip Poker*, *Film Strip*, and *Drag Strip*. Bartholomew, who has a psychotherapy practice in North Carolina, has written several other novels and another series.

Michael Lister's *Thunder Beach* also includes strip clubs and local bars, some fictional, some real. The mystery-thriller is set during Thunder Beach, the biannual motorcycle rally. The protagonist, a former reporter, while searching for a victim of sex trafficking, visits dozens of locations. The propeller from the *HMS Mica* that he hides behind is located in front of **Capt. Anderson's Restaurant and Maritime Market at 5551 N. Lagoon Dr., Panama City Beach**. Both *Miracle Strip* and *Thunder Beach* refer to **Thomas Drive**, the main drag; **Hathaway Bridge**, the Highway 98 bridge that connects Panama City and Panama City Beach; and **Historic St. Andrews**, a rejuvenated historic community with trendy restaurants and homes overlooking St. Andrews Bay. However, Tan Fannies, mentioned in both novels, met the hands of a wrecking ball in 2017. Lister also set his series featuring private eye Jimmy "Soldier" Riley in 1940s Panama City. The characters in several of Lister's *John Jordan* series often visit other Panama City restaurants and bars, including **Millie's Café at 228 Harrison Ave.** (See Wewahitchka, FL)

In *Beach Town*, a humorous mystery by *New York Times, USA Today,* and *Publishers Weekly* bestselling author Mary Kay Andrews (1954-), the main character travels to the Florida Panhandle in search of the perfect film location. As a movie location scout, the character is charged with finding a sleepy fishing village with an undiscovered beach town. For her quest, character Greer Hennessey begins in Panama City Beach, then explores Destin, Seaside, Rosemary Beach, WaterColor, Mexico Beach, and Apalachicola. In the end, the author invents the fictional town of Cypress Key, based on the real town Cedar Key. Mary Kay Andrews is the pen name of Kathy Hogan Trocheck, a St. Petersburg, Florida native. A former journalist, she now lives in Georgia, has written nearly thirty novels, and is often called the "Queen of the Beach Reads."

Writing under the pen name Michaela Thompson, Mickey Friedman (1944-) grew up along the beaches and swamps of Northwest Florida where she set three of her seven novels. Her *Panhandle Mystery* series includes *Hurricane Season, Riptide,* and *Heat Lightning,* which take place in the fictional town of St. Elmo. In another series, Friedman's main character is a reporter turned amateur detective named Georgia Lee Maxwell, who got her start at the small-town newspaper in Bay City. Friedman lives in New York but still spends time in the Panhandle.

Lake Alice in Wewahitchka, and its sister lake, Julia, are often mentioned in the John Jordan mysteries written by bestselling author Michael Lister. According to legend, the town gets its name from these lakes which resemble two watery "eyes." *Wewa* is a Seminole word for water.

WEWAHITCHKA, FLORIDA

This swampy, lake-bordered city about twenty-five miles east of Panama City is famous for one product, one movie, and one writer. *New York Times* and *USA Today* bestselling novelist and two-time Florida Book Award winner Michael Lister (1968-) lives in Wewahitchka and has set almost all of his thirty-plus books in the area.

Before Lister, however, Florida independent filmmaker Victor Nunez (1942-) brought Wewahitchka's gold to the silver screen. For over a hundred years, the Lanier family in this small town, population 1800, has been harvesting and packaging luscious, golden honey from the bloom of the tupelo tree, found in the nearby swamps. When Nunez saw a photograph of a beekeeper and a young girl, he was inspired to write the screenplay for *Ulee's Gold*. Nunez, now a professor at Florida State University in Tallahassee, chose Wewahitchka as the primary setting because he felt an authentic location was vital to telling the story. In the film, Peter Fonda stars as the aging, solitary beekeeper. Florida

beekeepers thought so highly of Fonda's performance they named him Florida Beekeeper of the Year in 1997. Ben Lanier, owner of L.L. Lanier & Sons Tupelo Honey worked with Nunez and Fonda on the making of the movie, filmed on location at Lanier's property. Tupelo honey is sold under various labels, but to buy the original Lanier honey like in the movie, buy from the Lanier family in Wewahitchka.

Honey and bees put Wewahitchka on the literary map. *Ulee's Gold,* an award-winning film, stars Peter Fonda as a beekeeper; Karen White's bestselling novel *Flight Patterns* includes a beekeeping motif. The Lanier family, who provided expertise for *Ulee's Gold,* still sells honey from their back porch in Wewahitchka.

To visit Wewahitchka from Panama City, drive east on Hwy. 98, then continue east on Hwy. 22.

An interesting literary detour off **Hwy. 22 leads to Gulf Correctional Institution, 500 Ike Steele Road,** the Florida prison featured in several novels written by bestselling author Michael Lister. To see the GCI, follow the highway marker and wind through the pine-dotted, middle-of-no-where countryside, veering to the left at the fork in the road, to dead end at GCI, a state-owned and operated prison with two units that can house up to 3000 inmates. Its austere presence offered little levity on my visit even though the

Despite its seasonal Halloween decorations at the entry, Gulf Correctional Institution is an austere place with a guard tower and prison buildings in the background. John Jordan, the prison chaplain protagonist in Michael Lister novels, solves murders while working here.

main entry sign outside the guardhouse was decorated for the holidays — Happy Halloween.

Before establishing himself as a writer, Michael Lister served as a prison chaplain for nearly a decade working out of "Wewa," as the locals call it. His most acclaimed series features John Jordan, a clerical detective and ecclesiastical sleuth, in this case – a prison chaplain. Though many of his mysteries are set in the fictional Potterville Prison, in the novel *Blood Oath*, the men's prison where character Chaplain John Jordan works is Gulf Correctional Institute.

Return to Hwy. 22 and continue east to visit Wewahitchka, the Chipola River, the Dead Lakes, and Lanier Honey. On the outskirts of town, Hwy. 22 passes between two lakes, Julia and Alice. Wewahitchka gets its name from the Native American words for these sister lakes. In Creek, *wewa* means water. According to legend, the lakes resemble two watery eyes. Both lakes are described in Michael Lister's novel *Beneath a Blood-Red Sky*. Character John Jordan's house overlooks Lake Julia, and the family frequents the park at Lake Alice. **Wewahitchka is at the intersection of Hwy. 22 and Hwy. 71. Turn left on Hwy. 71 to see Lake Alice or the Dead Lakes Recreation Area; turn right to visit Lanier Honey, Lake Julia, the Dead Lakes, and the Chipola River.**

Lanier Honey's official sales office is from a back porch in a residential section. **Turn right on Hwy. 71, go a few short blocks, then left onto Lake Grove Road. The house is in the third block, on the right at 318. Turn in the vine-covered driveway and wind around to the screened porch in**

Author Michael Lister flavors his novels with names of local cafés and restaurants. The Corner Café in Wewahitchka is a popular food stop for traveling readers as well as characters in his novels. It's near the crossroads of town at 108 N. Highway 71 across from Lake Alice.

The Chipola River provides an eerie setting for Florida novels with "dead" trees rising out of the water. A drive to the outskirts of Wewahitchka offers a glimpse into Old Florida bridges and rivers. The Chipola also has a 50-mile paddling trail offering a glimpse into springs, caves, and unspoiled natural Florida.

the back. There's a table set up with jars of honey. Someone will come out from the house to help you.

Continue on Lake Grove Road a few miles from Lanier Honey to see a wonderful panoramic vista of the Chipola River and the Dead Lakes from the old bridge spanning the Chipola River. Both sides of the approach to the bridge offer breathtaking views of swamps, with the "skulls" of dead trees hundreds of years old rising up through the water.

Several of the landings and houseboats along another part of the Chipola River provide interesting settings in Lister's novels. The author, according to his website, organizes River Readings, conferences with topics as creativity, spirituality, life, love, and relationships, to name a few. One such event was held at **Lister's Old Dairy Farm, 232 Wagon Wheel, on Dairy Farm Road, located off Hwy. 71 on the route to Port St. Joe.**

Lister also offers book readings and signings at local libraries. At Christmas time, he hosts an Annual Holiday New Book launch and reception at the **Northwest Regional Public Library, 898 W 11th St. in Panama City**.

His 2020 novel, *Beneath a Blood-Red Sky*, is rich in descriptions of the natural setting of the area – the Gulf, the bay, the swamps, with special attention to the Apalachicola River and the bluffs overlooking it. Lister's descriptions come to life when visiting local wildlife and environmental protection areas such as **National Estuarine Research Reserve in Apalachicola.** Though many of Lister's books are set in the fictional Potterville in Potter County, some like *A Certain Retribution* and *Beneath A Blood-Red Sky* are set solely in Wewahitchka.

THE FORGOTTEN COAST, FLORIDA

In the 1990s, this lonely stretch of Florida coastline was dubbed "The Forgotten Coast" when the chambers of commerce put on their collective thinking caps. The Forgotten Coast runs 200 miles along the coast from Mexico Beach around the bend, past Apalachicola around Apalachee Bay to Saint Marks. Unlike its high-rise condominium neighbors to the west, the waterfront villages are historic Old Florida-style. Here many of the residents still earn a living catching fish and harvesting oysters, though the oyster industry is on the wane. Both St. George and St. James, beautiful barrier islands with gorgeous beaches, are considered part of The Forgotten Coast. For the purposes of this book, sixty-five miles of The Forgotten Coast are still forgotten.

PORT ST. JOE, FLORIDA

The **Gulf County Sheriff's Office**, mentioned often in Michael Lister's books, is located at **418 Cecil G. Costin Sr. Blvd., Port St. Joe**. The office also shows up in another series of popular novels. Port St. Joe is also the setting for the three-book *Still Waters* suspense series co-written by Dawn Lee McKenna and Axel Blackwell.

The main character of the series, interim Sheriff Evan Caldwell, lives at the Port St. Joe Marina. The real marina where the fictional character lived and the Dockside Café where he ate grouper sandwiches were both destroyed by Hurricane Michael in 2018. Still standing, however, are **The Krazyfish Grille at 113 Monument** and **Cape San Blas Lighthouse**, listed on the National Register of Historic Places. Both are mentioned in *Dead Center*, the second book in the series. The lighthouse, relocated farther inland to Port St. Joe in 2014, is located at **George Core Park off Harborview Dr. on Miss Zola Road**. In *Dead Reckoning*, the first in the series, the acting sheriff investigates a body found in the **Dead Lakes**, about a mile north of Wewahitchka on **Florida Highway 71**.

Lister's novel *Blood Oath* includes mention of **No Name Books & Gifts, 325 Reid Ave.**, and gives a shout-out to the tacos from **Pepper's Mexican Restaurant**, a few doors up from the bookshop.

WATCH OUT FOR MOTORCYCLES

Twice a year, tens of thousands of bikers roll into Panama City Beach for Thunder Beach Motorcycle Rally, "the most biker-friendly free rally in the U.S."

Once a town with a thriving seafood industry, Apalachicola's shrimp boats and oyster shell mounds remain picturesque. The once-famous oyster industry provides unique settings and rich characters for regional authors. The State of Florida has closed commercial oystering in the area through 2025.

For the first time from Bay St. Louis to Apalachicola, travelers enter a different time zone. The Apalachicola River designates the Eastern Time Zone. This far south, Central Time changes where the Apalachicola River spills into the Intercoastal Waterway. Apalachicola is on Eastern time.

APALACHICOLA, FLORIDA

Author Dawn Lee McKenna endeared the town of Apalachicola with tens of thousands of readers. Reminiscent of Angela Lansbury's town in *Murder She Wrote*, "Apalach," as the locals call it, is an oyster and shrimping waterfront town with a New England feel.

McKenna's ten-book *Forgotten Coast* series takes place in Apalachicola and Port St. Joe. Occasional crimes send character Maggie Redmond of the Franklin County Sheriff's Department to nearby St. George Island. For another series set in the Florida Panhandle, McKenna created a fictional town of Dismal. McKenna, at times, used the names of real Apalachicola residents in the books – and they showed up at book signings to autograph books, signing copies right along with the author. In her books, McKenna wrote as if the town itself were a character. To bring it to life, she names real restaurants, bars, and even her favorite coffee shop, **Apalachicola Chocolate and Coffee Company at 75 Market.** She hosted book signings there until her death in 2021. It's still a cultural gathering spot with excellent coffee, handmade candies, event posters, and a little free library. When in town, McKenna also held book signings at what was then **Downtown Books & Purl at 67 Commerce,** a delightful independent bookstore with maps of literary Florida and plenty of books, both fiction and nonfiction, about the area. A bookshelf by the register, includes titles by local authors. McKenna, a native Floridian, relocated to Tennessee but visited Apalachicola often.

New York Times bestselling author Karen White (1964-) set her 2017 novel *Flight Patterns* in Apalachicola. In the mystery, the main character returns home to Apalachicola after a decade's absence. The author deftly takes the reader on walks around Apalachicola viewing the sites — along the waterfront, from parks to piers, to the **Margaret Key Library (80 12th St.),** and even the **John Gorrie Museum (46 6th St.).** Mentioned too are once-popular restaurants Boss Oyster and Caroline's which are attempting to reopen following devastation by Hurricane Michael. The author's descriptions of locations are so detailed, a reader can almost find the fictional house overlooking the bay where the main character's family lives, locate an abandoned house on

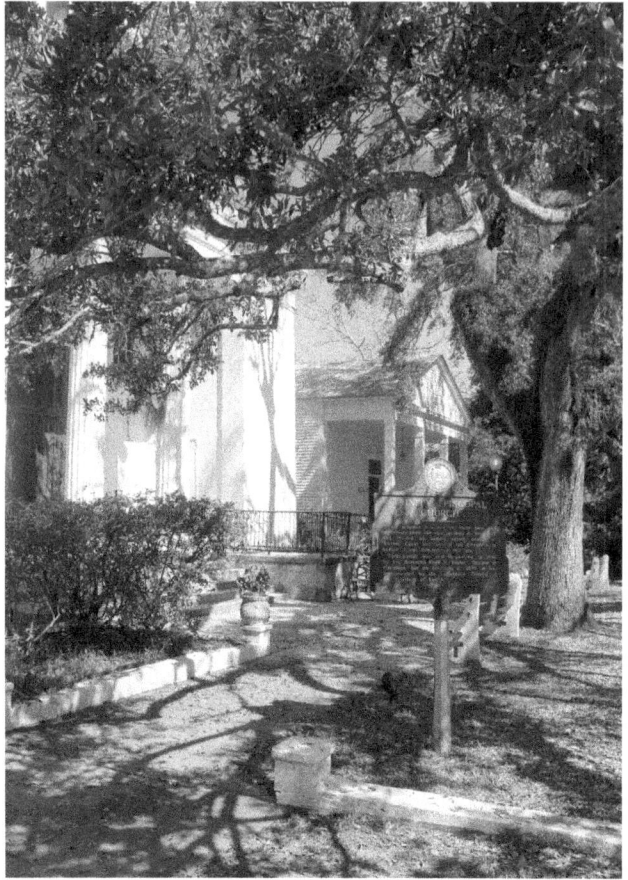

A short stroll around the Trinity Episcopal Church viewing historic markers, a museum, and a monument, recalls the landmarks described in Karen White's *Flight Patterns*. The church, established in 1837, is listed on the U.S. National Register of Historic Places.

a remote island near Eastpoint, or smell the exotic fragrance of the Pittosporum. The plot adds even more local color as it features beekeepers and tupelo honey. (See Wewahitchka, FL)

White, who resides part of the time in nearby WaterColor, has participated in Authors in Apalach, an annual event sponsored by the Apalachicola Margaret Key Municipal Library. The day-long festival held annually for twenty years, features book talks, author forums, sales, and book signings with as many as thirty authors, many of them award-winners with a local connection like White and Dawn Lee McKenna. The event is often held at the **Apalachicola Center for History, Culture and Art, 86 Water St.,** a historic cotton warehouse built in the 1830s. The **Margaret Key Library (80 12th St.)** houses a collection of Floridiana along with troves of local author treasures.

Novelist Claire Matturro's 2020 mystery *The Smuggler's Daughter* is set in Florida Panhandle, beginning in a fictional town near the Alabama line curving around the coastline to Apalachicola, where the main character faces

In 1930, author Marie Layet Sheip and her husband Stanley rented a cottage at 127 Bay Avenue. Later incorporated into the main house, the cottage was located on the rear of the property. The home began as a one-story in the late 1800s and has been restored and renovated several times. Below: A hundred years later, it still commands a beautiful bay view.

her troubled past in order to protect her future. Matturro, a prize-winning author, lawyer, and former professor, lives in Manatee County, Florida, and describes her latest books as "mysteries inspired by the beauty and insanity of Florida." The reader is reminded of Apalachicola's famous oyster industry when reading both Matturro's books and White's books set along The Forgotten Coast.

Mobile, Alabama, native Marie Layet Sheip (1885-1936), a silent screen writer and author of *Gulf Stream*, moved to Apalachicola with her husband Stanley, who managed a family-owned lumber business. She wrote the novel, considered literary fiction and a bestseller for its time, under the pen name Marie Stanley, a combination of their two first names. They rented what was probably the cottage (later joined with the main house) at the Cornelius Grady home on **127 Bay St**. in Apalachicola, now designatged as the **Grady-Hodges Home**. She and her husband later built a home at **915 Indian Pass Road at Indian Pass**, a small coastal community about **thirty minutes west of Apalachicola**. That house also still stands. She died in Apalachicola. (See Mobile, AL)

A visit to nearby **Apalachicola National Estuarine Research Reserve** will bring to life the power of the Apalachicola River as described in the novels of Michael Lister and other regional writers. To enjoy more scenery, cross the bridge to **Eastpoint** and drive around to view more of the terrain in Karen White's *Flight Patterns*. For a panoramic 360-degree view, climb the lighthouse at St. George Island and witness the waters that have inspired writers for centuries from Bay St. Louis to Apalachicola.

Just across the bridge from Apalachicola, St. George Island is home to a historic lighthouse and museum, natural dunes, and sparkling Gulf waters.

LONGITUDE, LATITUDE, GEOCACHE

In thousands of spots along the Gulf Coast, hidden treasures await the savvy seeker. Using the free Geocache app combined with a smart phone or GPS, treasure seekers can track down hidden "caches" in a technology-aided scavenger hunt. Of course, the hunt is the outdoor adventure itself since the treasures are usually small toys, trinkets, collectibles or geocoins. Treasure hunters locate the geocache using the device's display of longitude and latitude, plus occasional directions and hints.

Once geocachers find the cache, they sign a log, mark off the find, and may even add an item to the cache. Cities, counties, and states often encourage geocaching through parks and recreation departments. Some even offer commemorative reward tokens at the last cache. Some National Parks allow geocaching. GeoTours or GeoTrails are collective caches in one area, like a state park, to encourage visitors to explore while learning about the area via a treasure hunt.

Operation Recreation GeoTour is **Florida State Parks'** version; parks in **Pensacola** and on **St. George Island** are included. Florida even offers adult and kids cache hunts plus official, free reporting sites. The **City of Pensacola** has a geocache tour listed on its parks and recreation website.

Alabama State Parks offers a free geocaching permit if the park allows geocaching. More than 900 caches are hidden in the **Mobile** area alone.

Geocaching is allowed in **Mississippi State Parks**, though some have an admission fee. Typical hiding places include cultural centers, park benches, walking trails, lighthouses, and entrances to parks. Hiding places are rated on a difficulty level from 1 to 5. In "virtual" geocaches, a location rather than an item is discovered.

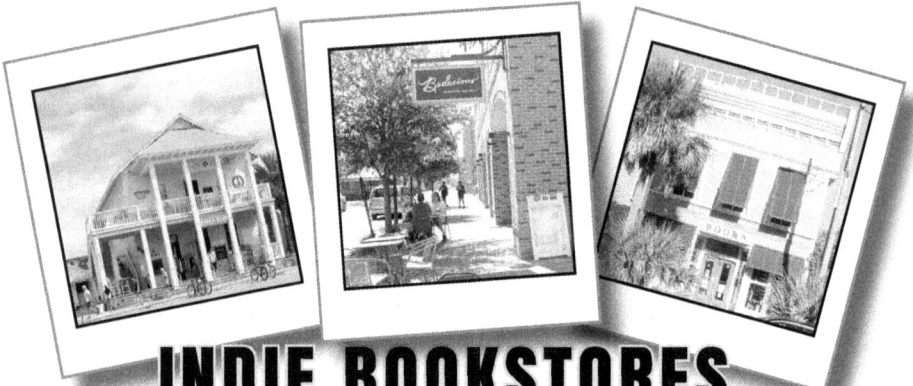

INDIE BOOKSTORES

PASS CHRISTIAN, MS - PASS CHRISTIAN BOOKS
300 E. SCENIC DR., (228) 222-4827

Located at Cat Island Coffeehouse, "Pass" Books is listed #8 on Americantown Media's Best Things Mississippi bookstores list. Operating since 2002, this two-story bookstore and coffee shop offers a deck overlooking the Gulf of Mexico and a second-floor loft devoted to Mississippi authors. They've hosted over 150 author events since 2016. In 2022 Robin Roberts started her newest book tour here, her hometown bookstore. One Book One Pass, the store's community sponsored reading project, encourages residents to read the same book each year to foster dialogue and promote reading. The store provides the high school with 300 complimentary copies of the title each year for junior and senior students.

MOBILE, AL - THE HAUNTED BOOK SHOP
9 S. JOACHIM ST., (251) 348-7668

USA Today bestselling paranormal author Angela Quarles owns this funky bookshop, re-established in 2018 and named after a popular Mobile bookstore owned by the author's grandmother which closed in 1991. The brick building is perfect for a "haunted" bookstore, with rough brick interior walls, stained concrete floors, nooks and crannies, curtained doorways, and ample display space. Complete with a bookstore cat, it carries both new and used books, plenty of books by local authors, a diversity of titles, and a fine children's collection.

FAIRHOPE, AL - PAGE & PALETTE
32 SOUTH SECTION ST., (251) 928-5295

Readers and writers for hundreds of miles around know this bookstore for its literary reputation. They've been selling books and art supplies since 1968 and continually expand their programs and facilities. The downtown location includes the Latte Da coffee bar and the Book Cellar, an event venue complete with beer, wine, and literary cocktails. Their reputation is so widespread, it's not surprising when they host a Pulitzer Prize winner for a book signing. Since 2005 they have sponsored One Town, One Tale, a community book read. Sometimes a local author is included. After all, more writers live in this area than probably any other place in America (per acre, that is). This bookshop even has a charitable foundation.

PENSACOLA, FL - BODACIOUS BOOKSTORE AND CAFÉ
110 EAST INTENDENCIA ST., (850) 446-6966

On street level under a posh downtown apartment complex, this bookstore is located, ironically, near where the old newspaper offices once stood. The bookstore, complete with café (beer, wine, and coffee too) opened in 2019 and has hosted numerous book signings and literary events. The store shelves a good selection of local authors' works and Discover Florida books, plus children's books and games. Around the corner from the bookstore is a bronze sculpture where visitors can pose for a photograph with an author-editor.

PENSACOLA, FL - OPEN BOOKS BOOKSTORE & PRISON PROJECT
1040 N. GUILLEMARD ST., (850) 453-6774

This nonprofit indie bookstore is popular with both locals and visitors. They stock new, pre-read and collectible books in a quaint, restored home near the historic North Hill neighborhood. They host author readings, book signings, well-known visiting authors, and several seasonal weekend-end book sales that draw thousands of shoppers. Open Books also offers an exceptional collection of academic books that scholars appreciate. For 25 years, they've been using book profits from the sale of books to enable the purchase and distribution of books to prisoners.

SEASIDE, FL - SUNDOG BOOKS
89 CENTRAL SQUARE, (850) 231-5481

Located in the heart of Seaside, this bustling bookstore is rated on Tripadvisor as the #1 thing to do in Seaside. For more than thirty years, the shady front porch with colorful Adirondack beach chairs has welcomed readers, browsers, and served as a stage for authors to sign their books. The store's inventory is selected by staff members rather than computer programs. Readers will find a diversity of nonfiction and fiction, especially in Southern literature and beach reads. In May, the shop is especially busy with events during the Longleaf Writer's Conference. There's a resident canine on the property (if he comes to work that day), hence the name Sundog, and yes, they sell T-shirts and coffee mugs. The second floor, where readers occasionally hide away, is home to Central Square Records, and, yes, they carry vinyl.

ROSEMARY BEACH, FL - HIDDEN LANTERN BOOKSTORE
84 N. BARRETT SQUARE, (850) 231-0091

This bookstore welcomes travelers, especially those staying for a while, and offers to set aside books for guests before their arrival. That's especially convenient for vacationers staying in one of the modern luxury lofts above the bookstore. The shop, which opened in 2011, features 15,000 titles. Their book signings introduce emerging writers and have welcomed big names like interior designers Verne Yip and James Farmer, and bestselling author Michael Lister. Be sure and look up at the chandeliers and hanging lanterns and browse the local author table by the front door.

PANAMA CITY , FL - BOOKISH BOUTIQUE
456 HARRISON AVE., (850) 320-8225

This pink bookstore offers a unique reader's experience in a delightful downtown location. The owner has transformed the old space and its brick walls, creating an alcove arch of books as a backdrop for authors reading their work or musicians performing at Friday night musical events. Along with new and used books and bookish accessories, they have a great line of apparel – sweatshirts and t-shirts – emblazoned with reading and book messages, plus popular prewrapped blind dates with a book.

PORT ST. JOE, FL - NO NAME BOOKS & GIFTS
325 REID AVE., (850) 229-9277

This one-time café now offers barista drinks, smoothies, free Wi-Fi plus a small but interesting inventory of new and used books, games, and puzzles in a cozy reading environment. No Name Books & Gifts is located on Port St. Joe's main drag and hosts occasional book signings.

APALACHICOLA, FL -OYSTERTOWN BOOKS
67 COMMERCE ST., (850) 653-1290

Tripadvisor ranks this downtown shop, formerly known as Downtown Books and Purl, as the #1 Place to Shop in Apalachicola. Located in a 100-year-old historic landmark building, the shop specializes in books by regional writers but houses plenty of other books. They also sell shirts, coastal merchandise, gift items, and the popular Blind Dates with a Book, including ones by local authors.

Day Trips

POETRY LOVER'S DAY TRIP
GULFPORT, MISSISSIPPI
READ • EAT • SEE

READ
"Billboards and Galleons" by Vachel Lindsay
Native Guard by Natasha Trethewey

EAT
Pack a picnic lunch or dine at the snack bar on
   Ship Island

or

Pick up po-boys to go from Pirate Cove, Robin
   Roberts' favorite po-boy place

SEE
Friendship Oak where Vachel Lindsay taught poetry
   to 1920s college girls (now University of Southern
   Mississippi at Gulf Park)
Beachfront across from USM where Lindsay walked
Ship Island replica lighthouse at Jones Park
   (catch ferry here)
Ship Island and Historic Fort Massachusetts
   Natasha Trethewey's inspiration for *Native Guard*
   (half-day trip on excursion ferry)

DAY TRIP
BILOXI, MISSISSIPPI
READ • EAT • SEE

READ

The Runaway Jury by John Grisham
Double Dog Dare by Gretchen Archer
Varina by Charles Frazier
"On the Mall," essay by Joan Didion

EAT

Mary Mahoney's Old French House,
    John Grisham's favorite restaurant

or

White Pillars, where Gretchen Archer orders
    Eggplant Josephine

SEE

Beau Rivage Casino's lobby and underground garage,
    Archer's cozy mystery setting

Beauvoir, home of writers Sarah Dorsey and
    Jefferson Davis (take the tour)

Edgewater Mall (on a rainy day)

KIDS' DAY TRIP
OCEAN SPRINGS, MISSISSIPPI
READ • EAT • SEE

READ
Smack Dab in the Middle of Maybe by Jo Hackl
The Secret World of Walter Anderson by Hester Bass

EAT
A picnic lunch like character "Cricket" or artist
   "Bob" would have eaten at Fort Maurepas
   City Park

SEE
Painted room, boat, bicycle, and art at
   Walter Anderson Museum of Art

History mural in Ocean Springs Community Center (part of Walter Anderson Museum of Art)

Painted theatre chairs with Anderson designs
   at Mary C. O'Keefe Cultural Arts Center

Ruskin Oak, the largest Live Oak in Mississippi

Shearwater Pottery where the Andersons
   still create pottery

DAY TRIP
MOBILE, ALABAMA
READ • EAT • SEE

READ

Seven Sisters by M. L. Bullock, book I in series
   inspired by Oakleigh House
"The Conquered Banner" by Father Abram Ryan,
   Civil War poet
St. Elmo by Augusta Evans, first woman writer
   to make $100,000

EAT

Callaghan's Irish Pub (look at the impressive little
   free library across the street) in Oakleigh Garden
   Historic District

SEE

Oakleigh Garden Historic District
Oakleigh House, take the tour
Father Ryan Park
Portier House where Father Ryan lived
Immaculate Conception Cathedral, site of Eugene
   Walter 's funeral
Ashland Place, historic district of gorgeous homes
   where streets are named for writers
Mobile Bay ferry to Fort Morgan where
   Augusta Evans nursed Civil War soldiers

DAY TRIP
POINT CLEAR & MAGNOLIA SPRINGS, ALABAMA
READ • EAT • SEE

READ

The All-Girl Filling Station's Last Reunion or *A Redbird Christmas* by Fannie Flagg

V for Victor by Mark Childress

Alabama Moon by Watt Key

EAT

Jesse's in Magnolia Springs, the village market and post office from time of Childress' book, now transformed into a restaurant

The Grand Hotel Golf Resort and Spa in Point Clear, dine like the characters in Fannie Flagg's books

SEE

Magnolia River Landing boardwalk, behind Jesse's, the river where the mail is still delivered by boat

Weeks Bay Estuarine Research Reserve & Pitcher Plant Bog, watch for birds from *A Redbird Christmas*

The Grand Hotel's back promenade overlooking Mobile Bay; look for the lighthouse, then visit the history center in the lobby

World's Once Smallest Library (drive by only)

DAY TRIP
SCENIC 30A, FLORIDA
READ • EAT • SEE

READ

From Beer to Eternity: A Chloe Jackson Sea Glass Saloon Mystery by Sherry Harris

Missing on 30A by Deborah Rine

Watch *The Truman Show*

EAT

Gourmet Food Trucks at Seaside

Have a fancy drink with a paper umbrella at a beach bar

SEE

Murals at Grayton Beach

Sundog Books

Truman House in Seaside

Shops at Rosemary Beach

READ

Beneath a Blood-Red Sky by Michael Lister
Dead Reckoning (Still Waters Suspense)
   by Dawn McKenna and Axel Blackwell
Flight Patterns by Karen White
Watch *Ulee's Gold*

EAT

Pepper's Mexican Grill, Port St. Joe
Coffee at No Name Books, Port St. Joe
Dessert at Apalachicola Chocolate & Coffee Co.

SEE

Gulf Correctional Institute, drive by
Lake Alice and Lake Julia, Wewahitchka
Honey at Lanier's Tupelo Honey, Wewahitchka
Shrimp boats, Apalachicola
Oystertown Books, Apalachicola
Grady House, 127 Bay, where Marie Layet Sheip lived,
   Apalachicola
National Estuary Research Reserve
Bridge to Eastpoint, St. George Island
   Lighthouse and Museum

THE SEARCH

Researching and writing in an age when countless information is published—almost simultaneously across numerous media—makes attribution challenging. I would like to acknowledge the numerous sources that served as springboards and inspiration in my quest to locate information on authors, the places of importance to them, and the significance of place in their works. I hope you'll also take note of the selected bibliography that follows.

I appreciate the local magazines like *Mobile Bay* and *Scenic 30A,* and lifestyle magazines like *Vie.* Journalistic endeavors like these don't always receive the reporting respect or recognition they deserve. These publications, along with real estate features, provided insight on local authors and histories of residences and neighborhoods.

Several websites provided invaluable information which made my endless research easier and credible. One online encyclopedia, *Mississippi Writers and Musicians*, was created by Starkville (Mississippi) High School English teacher Nancy Jacobs and researched by her students over a seven-year period. Even in retirement, Jacobs updates the site. For Alabama, *The Encyclopedia of Alabama* (operated by Auburn University Outreach and Alabama Humanities Alliance) answered almost any question about the state's historical writers. Another online source, *Alabama Writer's Forum*, a partnership program of the Alabama Council for the Arts, provided a valuable listing of contemporary authors for me to track down.

Municipal websites like BeautifulFairhope.com with its lists of Fairhope (Alabama) writers and City of Pascagoula (Mississippi) with its tour for bikers to pass by Jimmy Buffett sites and William Faulkner's marker were very helpful. City archives like those of Ocean Springs (Mississippi) helped me research famous residents of the past. The Hancock County (Mississippi) Historical Society shared photographs and information.

Contemporary authors' websites and their Facebook pages enabled me to learn about the writers firsthand and include their latest releases. The media and press kits offered on their websites provided reliable information. In some cases, Amazon author sites enhanced information.

Travel reviews and book reviews helped refresh my memory as I visited every place and read something by each author included in the book. I snapped photos of historical markers on location to document accuracy of these entries.

Google Maps (and good editors) helped me keep my compass straight when it came to writing directions. Snippets of Google books, The Gutenberg Project, and other online sites provided access to obscure books which have been digitized. Local librarians rushed to my rescue, especially those at the Hancock County-Bay St. Louis (Mississippi) Library and the Bay County Library in Apalachicola.

Tour guides, notably at Beauvoir in Mississippi and at Oakleigh House in Alabama, provided stories and factoids sparking my curiosity and sending me down another research rabbit hole — or two. Personnel at state welcome centers circled maps, charting my course. Even tourist information brochures added to my knowledge.

Danielle Davidson, former Education Specialist at Weeks Bay NERR, provided expertise, enthusiasm, and encouragement.

Susan Stein, historian of The Grand Hotel Golf Resort and Spa in Point Clear, Alabama, provided wonderful insight into the area's writers. History writer Pam Richardson of Apalachicola helped me verify where author Marie Sheip lived. I am also appreciative to the many other authors, curators, and historians who answered my emails and phone calls during the fact-checking stage of the book.

Booksellers, like the ones at Bay St. Louis' Bay Books (now closed), Seaside's Sundog Books, and Apalachicola's Downtown Books and Purl answered my questions, then fueled my literary curiosity. I left with bags of books to read.

Websites like Mappit with its "Books Set in Different Countries" and Wikipedia and Goodreads with categories of "writers by states" and "book places" were helpful. Facebook groups in several towns helped answer some of my questions. Followers at "Pascagoula, Remember when . . ." even provided a link to a photo of a Pulitzer Prize winner's home which was destroyed by Katrina. Craig Pittman's and Chadd Scott's podcast "Welcome to Florida" led me to some Florida writers new to me.

My subscription to Newspapers.com was worth every penny. I delighted in reading about Vachel Lindsay's public poetry readings in the 1920s, looking at the advertising for silent movies, their scripts written by Marie Layet, and reading Brad Watson's articles for the *Montgomery Advertiser*. Again, I felt like I was living in the authors' times by reading these digitized news stories, obituaries, and old-fashioned women's pages.

Some of my best tips came from family, friends, and fellow writers. They reminded me of things I'd forgotten, things I'd omitted, tracked down addresses and took photos, and then showered me with the gifts of new titles, new authors, and new places to pursue.

Acknowledgments

Writing a travel book during a pandemic posed some unexpected challenges, but family, friends, and fellow writers made my undertaking much easier. To them I am indebted.

Special thanks to my sons — Shannon for suggesting I narrow my writing scope to the Gulf South, Nick for adding film and music trivia, Colin for sharing the Seamark "family" logo; to my cousin Becky for coming on a Florida back roads trek to find a prison; and to my husband Danny for joining me on several scary road trips during COVID.

A special thank you to my dear friend Tookie (Marion) for being my traveling sidekick, backup photographer, part-time driver, and second set of eyes. She drove from Texas to Florida to help me explore Bay St. Louis, Ocean Springs, Point Clear, Pensacola, Apalachicola, and parts of The Forgotten Coast.

The Wednesday Portfolio group of Emerald Coast Writers encouraged, read, critiqued, edited, suggested, and proofed this manuscript for two years as membership ebbed and flowed during the pandemic. Thank you to Charlie, Jeannie, Pat, Patrick, Patty, Susan, Heather, Candy, Tom, Lucie, Judy, and those who joined us briefly. You each offered a special skill from fact-checking to cheerleading to sharing your travel experiences. All were invaluable.

And to Mandy, who offered courage, feedback, and editorial support — thank you for helping me create a better book for readers and travelers.

A big thank you to my neighbor Christy who told me about a literary gem in Westville and who helped edit and proofread the manuscript.

To authors Pat Black-Gould, Charlie Davis, Susan Feathers, and Jeannie Zokan, thank you for previewing my book and allowing me to use your descriptions on the back cover.

It's been a wonderful writing journey with family, friends, and fellow writers.

Any errors or omissions are entirely mine. My support team is flawless!

Thank you!

Select Bibliography

Alabama Writers' Forum. "Contemporary Alabama Authors Directory." https://www. writersfo rum.org/resources/authors/

Anderson, Walter Inglis, and Redding S. Sugg. *The Horn Island Logs of Walter Inglis Anderson*. Memphis, TN: Memphis State Univ. Press, 1973.

Archer, Gretchen. *Double Agent: A Davis Way Crime Caper*. Frisco, TX: Henery Press, 2019.

———. *Double Dog Dare*. Frisco, TX: Henery Press, 2018.

Beautiful Fairhope Alabama. http://beautifulfairhope.com/about/fairhope-authors/

Beck, Allisa L. *Long Beach*. Charleston, SC: Arcadia Publishing, 2015.

Birnbaum, Robert. "Brad Watson." Identity Theory. Duende Publishing, July 21, 2002. http://www. identitytheory.com/brad-watson.

Boehm, Colette. "Delivering on the River." *Alabama Living Magazine*. Alabama Rural Electric Co operative, June 5, 2020. https://alabamaliving.coop/articles/delivering-on-the-river/.

"Books by Mickey Friedman and Complete Book Reviews." PublishersWeekly.com. *Publishers Weekly,* August 5, 1988. https://www.publishersweekly.com/pw/authorpage/mickey-friedman.html.

"Books to Read on Vacation by Local Destin and 30A Authors – Five Star Properties." Five Star Properties Destin/30A. Five Star Properties, February 22, 2018. https://www.fivestargulfrentals. com/blog/books-to-read-on-vacation-destin-florida-authors/.

Bowden, Jesse Earle. *Gulf Islands: The Sands of All Time: Preserving America's Largest National Sea shore*. Fort Washington, PA: Eastern National, 1994.

Broom, Brian. "Tom Kelly, Author of Tenth Legion, Harvests Mississippi Turkey at 94 Years Old." *Mississippi Clarion Ledger*. March 26, 2022.

Buffett, Jimmy. *The Pirate Looks at 50*. New York, NY: Random House Large Print, 1998.

City of Panama City Beach, FL. Area Information. (n.d.). Retrieved June 23, 2022, from https:/ www.pcbfl.gov/about-us/visitors/area-information

City of Pascagoula, MS. https://cityofpascagoula.com/194/Parks-Facilities

Davis, Margaret. "Program History and Writer-in-Residence Wolff Cottage." Fairhope Center for the Writing Arts. FCWA, 2004. https://www.fairhopecenterforthewritingarts.org/.

De Priest, Joe. "New Insights on the South's Poet Priest." Newspapers.com. *Charlotte Observer,* August 31, 2003. https://www.newspapers.com/image/630686888/?terms=father+abram+ry an&match=1.

DeLeon, Thomas C. *Belles, Beaux and Brains of the 60's.* New York, NY: G.W. Dillingham Co, 1909.

Donelson, Cathy. *Images of America: Fairhope*. Charleston, SC: Arcadia Publishing, 2005.

Ericson, Sally Pearsall. "A Famous Mobilian You Should Know: William March, Author of 'The Bad Seed'." Al, March 13, 2014. https://www.al.com/living/2014/03/a_famous_mobilian_you_should_k.html

———. "Cool Spaces: Two Historic Homes Showcase Flair of Ashland Place Neighborhood." AL.com. September 24, 2014.

"Eugene Walter, 76, a Novelist of the South." *The New York Times.*, April 26, 1998. https://www.nytimes.com/1998/04/26/nyregion/eugene-walter-76-a-novelist-of-the-south.html.

"Eugene Walter: Last of the Bohemians." Alabama Public Broadcasting, 2008.

Evans, Augusta Jane. *St. Elmo.* New York, NY: Co-operative Publication Society, 1866.

Flagg, F. (2004). *A Redbird Christmas.* Random House, Inc.

———. "Fannie Flagg's Fairhope." *Garden & Gun*, April 5, 2017.

———. (2014) *The All-Girl Filling Station's Last Reunion: A Novel.* New York, NY: Random House.

Flores, Sarah. "Author Interview – Dawn Lee McKenna." Write Down the Line. LLC Book Ed Editing, April 24, 2020. https://www.writedowntheline.com/post/interview-author-dawn-lee-mckenna-1.

Ford, Jennifer. "Prentiss Ingraham: King of the Dime Novel." University of Mississippi Libraries - Ingraham exhibition. University of Mississippi. Accessed April 17, 2022. https://olemiss.edu/depts/general_library/archives/exhibits/past/ingrahamex/ingraham.html.

Foreman, Josh, and Ryan Starrett. (2019) *Hidden History of the Mississippi Sound.* Charleston, SC: The History Press.

Franke, Damon. "Vachel Lindsay at Gulf Park, 1923 to 1924." *Mississippi Quarterly* 69, no. 4 (2016): 433–56. https://doi.org/10.1353/mss.2016.0001.

Frazier, Charles. *Varina.* New York, NY: Hodder & Stoughton, 2018.

Gray, Charles H. *Bay St. Louis, Mississippi: Celebrating the First 300 Years.* Bay St. Louis, MS: Hancock County Historical Society, 1998.

Gulf Breeze UFO. You Tube, 2007. https://www.youtube.com/watch?v=9AaIl-vHIns&t=7s.

Hackl, Jo. *Smack Dab in the Middle of Maybe.* New York, NY: Yearling, 2019.

Haines, Carolyn. *Judas Burning.* Blue Ash, OH: Tyrus Books, 2012.

Harkey, Ira B. *The Smell of Burning Crosses.* Jacksonville, IL: Harris-Wolf, 1967.

Harris, Sherry. *Chloe Jackson, Sea Glass Saloon Mystery: From Beer to Eternity.* New York, NY: Kensington Books, 2020.

Higginbotham, Jay. *Pascagoula; Singing River City.* Mobile , AL: Gill Press, 1967.

Jackson, Joshilyn. *Never Have I Ever: A Novel.* New York, NY: William Morrow, 2021.

Jumper, Kathy. "Pulitzer to Bring Pulitzer Hotel to Fairhope ." *Press Register* AL.com, March 20, 2011.

Kava, Alex. *Lost Creed.* Omaha, NE: Prairie Wind Publishing, 2018.

Kazek, Kelly. "Fannie Flagg's Quirky Alabama: 7 Real Oddities and Attractions in Her Books." AL.com, November 13, 2013.

Key, Watt. "The Point Clear Library." *Mobile Bay Magazine,* July 2017.

Lanier, L. L. and Sons Tupelo Honey. https://www.lltupelohoney.com/ulees-gold. Accessed April 20, 2022.

Lister, Michael. *Beneath a Blood-Red Sky.* Charleston, SC: Pulpwood Press, 2020.

Matthews, Michelle. "Celebrated Romance Writer Opening New Bookstore in Mobile." *Press Register* www.AL.com. May 30, 2018.

Matturro, Claire Hamner. *The Smuggler's Daughter.* Garner, NC: Red Adept Publishing, 2020.

McCaddon, Beauvals. "Depression's Bright Side." Review of The House of Percy: Honor, Melancholy, and Imagination in a Southern Family," *Tallahassee Democrat,* (December 25, 1994).

McKenna, Dawn Lee, and Axel Blackwell. *Dead and Gone.* Middleton, DE: Sweet Tea Press Publication, 2019.

———. *Dead Center: Still Waters Suspense.* Middleton, DE: Sweet Tea Press Publication, 2018.

———. *Dead Reckoning: A Still Waters Suspense Novel.* Middleton, DE: Sweet Tea Press Publication, 2017.

McPhail , Carol. "Father Abram J. Ryan: Poet, Priest, Defender of the South (Photos)." Al.com. Alabama Media, March 22, 2013. https://www.al.com/living/2013/03/father_abram_ryan_poet-priest.html.

Miller, Mike. "Florida Road Trip: Old Towns on the Forgotten Coast." *Florida Back Roads Travel,* March 13, 2022. https://www.florida-backroads-travel.com/old-florida-towns-on-the-forgotten-coast.html?fbclid=IwAR3x5BnbGUsQm8Slilncpoq7pb4enPZQmyWUh2Bw. Updated March 13, 2022.

Mississippi Writers & Musicians. https://www.mswritersandmusicians.com/mississippi-writers. Mississippi Writers Project, Starkville, MS.

Myers, Craig. "I saw UFO photos faked, witness says." *Pensacola News Journal,* June 17, 1990.

National Estuarine Research Reserves. https://coast.noaa.gov/nerrs/

O'Brien, Ben. "The Legend of Col. Tom Kelly." MeatEater Hunting. *MeatEater,* June 7, 2019. https://www.themeateater.com/hunt/wild-turkey/the-legend-of-col-tom-kelly.

Pittman, Craig. *Oh, Florida!: How America's Weirdest State Influences the Rest of the Country.* New York, NY: St. Martin's Press, 2016.

The Portier House: A Property of the Archdiocese of Mobile, Guided Tour Brochure. Accessed April 16, 2022. https://mobilecathedral.org/the-portier-house.

Potts, Jocko. "E. O. Wilson's Mobile." *Mobile Bay Magazine*, December 28, 2021. Reprint 2010 article.

Revisiting The Gulf Breeze UFO Sightings: A YouTube Documentary. Holden Hardman, 2021. https://www.youtube.com/watch?v=pJzLKIqp-3w.

Richardson, Pam. "Chasing Shadows: Novelist Wrote '30s Bestseller in Apalachicola." *The Apalachicola Times.* February 11, 2022. https://www.franklincounty.news/stories/novel ist-wrote-30s-bestseller-in-apalachicola.

———. "The Grady-Hodges House: 127 Bay Avenue, Apalachicola, Florida," January 2020.

Rideout, Walter B. *Sherwood Anderson a Writer in America.* 1. Vol. 1. Madison, WI: University of Wisconsin Press, 2007.

Roberts, Robin. *Everybody's Got Something: A Memoir.* New York, NY. Grand Central Publishing, 2014.

Ryan, Abram Joseph. "Father Ryan's Poems: Ryan, Abram Joseph, 1839-1886," Free Download, Borrow, and Streaming." Internet Archive. Mobile, J. L. Rapier & co, January 1, 1879. https:/ archive.org/details/fatherryanpoems00ryanrich/page/n29/mode/2up.

Sloan, W. David, and Laird B. Anderson. *Pulitzer Prize Editorials: America's Best Editorial Writing, 1917-1993.* Ames, IA: Iowa State University Press, 1994.

Smith, Frank. "Sarah Dorsey's Life Paints Pictures of the Old South." *Clarion-Ledger.* January 12, 1989.

Spiegel, Brendan. "'Travel: A Southern Town That's Been Holding onto Its Charm for More Than Century.'" *New York Times*, March 1, 2019. www.nytimes.com.

Tucker, Jennifer. "Gulf Breeze UFOs: Controversy Hangs Over UFO Town." *Tampa Tribune*, January 29, 1989.

Turk, Marilyn. *Rekindled Light.* Forget Me Not Romances, 2019.

University of Alabama Libraries. "This Goodly Land." Marie Stanley. University of Alabama Libraries. Accessed April 16, 2022. https://apps.lib.ua.edu/blogs/this-goodly-land/author/?AuthorID=81.

University of West Florida Historic Trust. https://uwf.edu/university-advancement/departments/historic-trust/ Pensacola, FL.

Van Camp, April. "Nancy Bartholomew: Panhandle Mystery Writer." Essay. *In Florida Crime Writers: 24 Interviews,* edited by Steven Glassman, 7–13. Jefferson, NC: McFarland, 2007.

Visit Florida. "How to Tour the Great Florida Birding Trail's Northwest Section." Visit Florida, July 27, 2021. https://www.visitflorida.com/travel-ideas/articles/outdoors-nature-great-flori da-birding-trail/.

WMBB News. "Panama City Beach: The history of the Spring Break Capital of the World."
YouTube. Retrieved June 23, 2022, from https://www.youtube.com/watch?v=bmBwkH--WdI.

Walter, Eugene, and Katherine Clark. *Milking the Moon: A Southerner's Story of Life on This Planet.*
New York, NY: Crown Publishers, 2001.

Walters, Ed, and Frances Walters. *The Gulf Breeze Sightings.* New York, NY: William Morrow
& Co. Inc., 1990.

Ward, Jesmyn. *Salvage the Bones.* London, UK: Bloomsbury, 2013.

Webb, Paula, "Madame Le Vert: Hostess Extraordinaire." *Mobile Bay Magazine.* PMT Publish
ing, July 26, 2018. https://mobilebaymag.com/madame-le-vert-hostess-extraordinaire/.

Welcome to Florida: Episode 89 "Florida Mysteries." Apple Podcasts. Welcome to Flor
ida, 2022. https://podcasts.apple.com/us/podcast/episode-89-cozy-florida-mysteries/
id1519841529?i=1000553293624.

White, Karen. *Flight Patterns.* New York, NY: Penguin Group USA, 2017.

Williams, Tennessee, and Thomas Keith. *A House Not Meant to Stand: A Gothic Comedy.* New York,
NY: New Directions, 2008.

Zokan, Jeannie. Personal communication. June 26, 2022.

GENERAL INDEX SEE ALSO: Author Index, Book Index, Town Index

AUTHOR INDEX

*Pseudonyms or also known as

BOOK INDEX

TOWN INDEX

About the Author

DIANE JONES SKELTON is an author, journalist, former educator, and award-winning feature writer with a passion for literature, travel, and photography. As an educator, she co-authored *Dickens to Dialysis: The How-To of Interdisciplinary Field Trips*, a travel guide for secondary teachers in Texas. As a journalist, she wrote a weekly column, "Traipsin' Around," a travel column for an East Texas publication, *Tyler Country*.

She is a frequent contributor to travel review site Tripadvisor. In 2017 she researched and created the humorous brochure "Weird Pensacola" for Foo Foo Festival's "Funny Side of Florida" events hosted by West Florida Literary Federation. She also managed "Viva Florida 500!" quincentennial events for the writing community in the Pensacola area.

Academically, her work has been published in *The English Journal* and national fraternal publications. Her feature articles have appeared in regional publications as *Mississippi Magazine, Florida Hockey Life*, and *Emerald Coast Review*, and in newspapers such as *The Gulf Breeze News*. She advised award-winning student publications in Louisiana, Texas, and Kansas. Along with teaching journalism, photojournalism, and literature in high schools in Louisiana and Texas, she taught Mass Communications at Tarrant County College in Fort Worth, and advised the magazine and newspaper at Washburn University in Kansas.

Her WordPress blog, *The Gumbo Diaries*, showcases articles on literary travel and writers, both contemporary and classic. She has published two memoirs, *The Gumbo Diaries: Mississippi and Beyond* (2015) and *Thanks for Asking* (2020). She teaches memoir classes at the Gulf Breeze, Florida, Senior Center and facilitates writing groups in the Pensacola area. She is a member of National League of American Pen Women, Florida Writers Association, and Emerald Coast Writers.

A native of Pascagoula, Mississippi, she holds a B.S. in Journalism and English from the University of Southern Mississippi and a Master's in Journalism from the University of Kansas. She lives with her family in Gulf Breeze, Florida, midway (almost) between Bay St. Louis and Apalachicola.

www.ingramcontent.com/pod-product-compliance
Lightning Source LLC
LaVergne TN
LVHW051102080426
835508LV00019B/2012